BODY DRIFT

CARY WOLFE, SERIES EDITOR

(continued on page 165)

BODY DRIFT

BUTLER, HAYLES, HARAWAY

ARTHUR KROKER

posthumanities 22

University of Minnesota Press
Minneapolis
London

Published by the University of Minnesota Press
111 Third Avenue South, Suite 290
Minneapolis, MN 55401-2520
http://www.upress.umn.edu

Library of Congress Cataloging-in-Publication Data
Kroker, Arthur.
Body drift : Butler, Hayles, Haraway / Arthur Kroker.
(Posthumanities; 22)
Includes bibliographical references and index.
ISBN 978-0-8166-7915-7 (hc : alk. paper)
ISBN 978-0-8166-7916-4 (pb : alk. paper)
1. Human body (Philosophy). 2. Feminist theory. 3. Feminist criticism. 4. Butler, Judith. 5. Hayles, Katherine.
6. Haraway, Donna Jeanne. I. Title.
B105.B64K76 2012
128'.6—dc23
2012030017

19 18 17 16 15 14 13 12   10 9 8 7 6 5 4 3 2 1

CONTENTS

ACKNOWLEDGMENTS

I am deeply appreciative of the Social Sciences and Humanities Research Council of Canada for research support (Digital Inflections) that was vital to the completion of this manuscript. My appointment as a Canada Research Chair in Technology, Culture, and Theory at the University of Victoria represents a form of long-term intellectual support that has made interdisciplinary projects of this order possible.

The insightful comments provided by reviewers for the University of Minnesota Press as well as by the Faculty Editorial Committee were very helpful in preparing the manuscript for publication. I gratefully acknowledge Cary Wolfe's intellectual encouragement in enabling *Body Drift* to be part of the Posthumanities series at the University of Minnesota Press. As always, discussions with Marilouise Kroker have shaped the critical direction of my thought on bodies and power.

1

BODY DRIFT

Body drift is everywhere in culture and society.

Though it was anticipated that the speed and intensity of techno-logical change would effectively marginalize concern with the body, highlighting the digital rather than the corporeal, subordinating human flesh to data flesh, quite the opposite has occurred. Images of the corporeal body are the key visual language of contemporary politics. We may live in the shadow of an empire of cyber-power with what the German theorist Peter Sloterdijk has described as "terror from the air," but the messianic goals of "total information warfare" are effectively stymied by bombs strapped to bodies of religious and political fighters, whether in the markets of Pakistan, the streets of Baghdad, the parched hills of Afghanistan, or the subways of Moscow. While the triumph of mass media, particularly television, may portend a future of pure simulation, the overrid-ing cultural reality is that the image machine is itself haunted by memories of the body: bodies of missing children; crime victims; bodies of those abused, violated, accidented, disappeared. While the privileged language of genomics might anticipate a future of delirious genetic engineering, the political reality today is that the future of genomics is itself challenged by religious concerns with the sanctity of the body. Of course, the rise of religious fundamen-talism is itself challenged in turn by the new body politics of gays, lesbians, transsexuals, and transgendered persons.

We are literally drifting through many different specular per-formances of the body, from the reactionary to the progressive, but for that, all commonly transformational, all evoking the sign of the body as a fateful talisman of that which must be alternatively protected, forbidden, sheltered, transgressed, emancipated. There is no longer, if there ever was, a single, binding, universal history of the body, nor is it possible to speak today of the body as a cohesive singularity. Indeed, if so many issues related to bodily politics can inflect public space and private time, it is because the very meaning, both surfaces and structure, of the body has begun to drift. Body drift refers to the fact that we no longer inhabit *a* body in any meaningful sense of the term but rather occupy a multiplicity of bodies—imaginary, sexualized, disciplined, gendered, laboring, technologically augmented bodies. Moreover, the codes governing behavior across this multiplicity of bodies have no real stability but are themselves in drift—random, fluctuating, changing. There are no longer fixed, unchallenged codes governing sexuality, gender, class, or power but only an evolving field of contestation among different interpretations and practices of different bodily codes. The multiplicity of bodies that we are, or are struggling to become, is invested by code-perspectives. Never fixed and unchanging, code-perspectives are always subject to random fluctuations, always evolving, always intermediated by other objects, by other code-perspectives. We know this as a matter of personal autobiography. For all the hype surrounding discussions of the extropian bodies of technological futurism, who has not had the experience of drifting within her own bodily history, selectively but no less intensely remembering past events, measuring past against present and future, drifting episodically, randomly, between the pull of social networking technologies and the always constraining push of individual autobiography? Body drift is how we circulate so effortlessly from one medium of communication to another; it is how we explore intimately and with incredible granularity of detail the multiplicity of bodies that we have become; it is how our bodies are inflected, intermediated, complicated. It is a double movement, then: we drift within and across the multiplicity of our own bodily inflections; and the multiplicity of bodies that we have become—the who we are and what we would like to be—is itself caught up in a larger, more heterogeneous current of code drift. Indeed, to the question, What allows the body to be such a broad category of analysis and, at the same time, not to have any apparent coherence? it might be responded that it is precisely the lack of coherence on the part of the body that is the essential, constitutive condition for the specter of the body to continue to circulate as a phantasmagoric sign of putative unity. In this case, the body can inflate as a universal sign of equivalence precisely to the extent that the *actual* meaning of the body has radically dispersed. Circuited by all the flows of power, patterned by codeworks, shaped by norms of cultural intelligibility, an object of viral invasion, with its subjectivity increasingly taking the form of possessed individualism, the body can acquire such a powerful epistemological presence as a universal sign because the bodies that we are or would like to become are themselves increasingly dispersed, intermediated, unfinished, spliced, straining.

Nothing is as imaginary as the material body. Circulating, fluid, borderless, with no certain boundaries or predetermined history, the body has no meaning today other than its intermediations, no autobiography that does not possess its own hauntologies, and certainly no drift that does not leave a trace of its presence. There definitely are codes of gender that can be transgressed only at the price of punishment, but there are always gender drifters who remix, recombine, and resplice the codes of gender performance. There certainly is a disciplinary regime of sexuality, but there are also sex-code drifters who make of their own sexual assignment an opportunity to transgress the codes, to refuse the normative, to overcome the predetermined. Against class inequities burned into disciplined, laboring bodies, there are class drifters who make of their own protesting, rebelling, insurgent bodies a marker of the struggle for freedom. While the age of specialization resulted in the definitive separation of the senses, body drift begins with a grand unification of the human sensorium.

In genomics, new scientific theories focused on "genetic drift" support an image of the body deeply influenced by random fluctuations, shaped by accidental events, and inflected by the vicissitudes of material history. In the artistic imagination, representational depictions of the bounded body of modernist times have been challenged by images of bodies circulating, crossing boundaries, in flux with no definite purpose or certain direction. In cinema, body drift is the visual essence of powerful visualization of bodies of the future, with their complex intermediations of code, flesh, and desire. Interpolated by ideology, addressed by power, circulating within the image vectors of mass media, mobilized within vast data archives, and, at all times and places, deeply inflected by questions of gender, sexuality, race, and class, the body today knows only drift in its mediated surfaces and deepest biological structures. Always circulating at the edge of codes old and new, knowing no certain boundaries, never simply a product of gender construction or essential identity, body drift is our real technological autobiography.

That contemporary body politics focuses today with such elemental ferocity on highly contested attempts to freeze the circulation of bodies, codes, and histories is probably motivated in large part by the actual, objective presence of body drift as the animating energy of culture and society. The political theorist Wendy Brown has evocatively described our current politics as powerfully marked by "states of injury," namely, by powerful psychological reaction-formations generated by deep and lasting attachments to anger from any perceived attempts to cross sexual borders, imagine new genders, or remix bodily codes.[1] The anger directed today against body drift is palpable, diffuse, and often violent. It has, of course, its privileged targets: same-sex marriage; the bodily politics of gays, lesbians, transgenders, and transsexuals; stem cell research; reproductive rights debates. Sometimes assuming the electoral form of Proposition 8 campaigns in California, aimed at preserving the rights of heterosexual normativity, at other times adopting restrictive measures aimed at marginalizing the sudden proliferation of countersexualities, seemingly in country after country marked by strikingly reactionary attempts to maintain the masculine as the universal signifier, body drift is under attack.

And well it might be. Both symptomatic sign and precondition of a fundamentally new way of understanding the body, the specter of body drift is a very real threat to defenders of ideological purity. More than a panic response to the sudden collapse of images of the body bound up with an *idée fixe* from the normative regimes of religion, politics, or gender, the circulation of imaginary bodies that is the essence of body drift provokes in its wake the most bitter of cultural backlash. After all, crashing boundaries open up new possibilities, but they also aggravate the most recidivist feelings, attitudes, and perspectives. But for all that, body drift cannot really be stopped. It is constituted by the blast of information culture, envisioned by artists, implicitly communicated by social networking technologies, signified by those ineffable signs of body drift—tattoos, rings, and scarification—and lived daily by remixing, resplicing, and redesigning codes: codes of gender, sexuality, class, ideology, identity. But most of all, body drift has its key theorists—Judith Butler, N. Katherine Hayles,[2] and Donna Haraway—whose writings provide the vocabulary so desperately required to understand the contingencies, complexities, and intermediations of body drift.

Contingency, Complexity, and Hybridity

Taken together, the writings of Butler, Hayles, and Haraway provide a coherent, critical, and eloquent account of body drift: its hauntologies, complexities, and intermediations. Their theorizations of the body in its complicated inflections with the languages of gender, sexuality, science, ideology, power, and politics are never reducible to description but are actually part of the discourse of the body—not as ideological prefiguration but in the subtler sense that their theoretical imaginations are directly invested in the fate of the body. To engage with their writings is to be caught up in the language of body drift itself, exploring from within the often hidden traces of gender construction, passionately invested in the struggle for bodies that matter, understanding that the stakes of debates in cognitive science are nothing less than the future of posthuman bodies, finally leaving behind the anthropomorphic foundations of species-logic to join that spectacular trajectory represented in all its enigmatic promise by the term *companion species*.[3] Indeed, if the theoretical constructions of Butler, Hayles, and Haraway capture so powerfully the essential currents of body drift, if their reflections crystallize the implosion of tightly scripted bodily regimes followed by the swift emergence of body drift—deconstructed genders, hybrid species, circulating desire, mobilized identities—this may originate in the fact that each thinker represents a very different, yet complementary, theoretical inflection.

Contingency

For example, Judith Butler literally enacts in the eloquence and precision of her writings a theory of the contingent body, its disavowals, hauntologies, repressions, and possible reflexivity. Focused at first on the disciplinary regimes associated with "compulsory heterosexual normativity," Butler no sooner deconstructs scenes of identity misrecognition in *Gender Trouble* and *Bodies That Matter* than her thought is itself caught up in the larger drift of power and its resistances.[4] In texts ranging from *Antigone's Claim, The Psychic Life of Power, Giving an Account of Oneself, Undoing Gender,* and *Precarious Life,*[5] her theoretical imagination travels well beyond the domain of heterosexual normativity, touching directly on issues of mourning and violence, with all their disavowals and politics of ressentiment. Everywhere in her writings, there is something resembling a faithful reenactment of what she once described as the "shameless impurity" of Antigone, a passionate evocation of that which is vulnerable, unintelligible, unknowable, unrepresentable in the human condition. Here the body is performed in its full multiplicity: performing gender, ideology, reflexivity, melancholic subjectivity, and compulsory heterosexual normativity. As well it must be since Butler's overall thesis has everything to do with hauntologies of body drift, with the elemental fact that bodies are always between living and dying, forever destabilized between the social claims of heterosexual normativity and political ambitions toward "critical desubjectivation." For all her hopeful focus on strategies, which take advantage of any and all failures of inter-pellation, Butler remains a realist on the enduring presence in bodily politics of a passionate attachment to subjection. Of course, many philosophers have gone this way before: Hegel's *unhappy consciousness,* Freud's *melancholic ego,* Althusser's *interpellation,* Nietzsche's *bad conscience.* Yet Butler pursues the why of our pas-sionate attachment to subjection with such relentlessness that the body is forced finally to confess that it is possessed—indeed, structured—by an "unconscious of power," one that operates by turning back on itself as both origin and destination. When Butler writes *Precarious Life: Powers of Mourning and Violence,* what is at stake is not only a critical reflection on the presence of Heidegger's "abuse value" in contemporary politics—ethnic scapegoating, in-definite detention, disappearances, and oppressions—but a more pessimistic assessment that the unconscious of power may, in the end, be resistant to strategies of reflexivity. But if the politics of compulsory heterosexuality, with its phantasmatic identification, reveals itself to be fully proximate to power, this can only mean that resistance to such compulsion can *only* take the form of body drift: queering bodies, ideology, politics, gender. Literally, the act of bringing into presence melancholic disavowals represents an opportunity for finally *undoing* the phantasmatic body.

Consequently, it is to the language of psychoanalysis (the incest taboo, bodily confession, the end of sexual difference) as well as to the question of the philosophy of sexuality itself (the limits of sexual autonomy, longing for recognition, gender regulations, letting the other of philosophy speak) that she turns—turns, that is, both to reassert the deconstructive spirit of *Gender Trouble* and rethink in a new key the basic theses of *Bodies That Matter*: in her texts, what it might mean for that which has been excluded—transexuality, intersexuality, transgendered persons—to be included, not only in the normativity of society but, more to the point, in the regime of truth of feminist and queer theory. After all, like every discourse, feminist and queer theory has its particular regimes of truth, its discursive limits that are rigorously policed, and on behalf of which, both have often been reluctant to undo the question of gender in a way that would be receptive to the claims of what is perceived as a *mauvais plis*—the third term of sexuality—in such a way that the revolt of the third term of sexuality, neither pure male or pure female but intersexual, transsexual, transgendered, also destabilizes the narrative of modernity. Here gender assignment is also a way of keeping intact the ruling political binaries. When gender begins to drift, when the contingency of the body can no longer be contained within the deconstructive terms of *Gender Trouble* or the aporias of *Bodies That Matter,* what occurs in Butler's thought is a fateful inflection of gender in the direction of an ethics of kinship *(Antigone's Claim)*, moral philosophy *(Giving an Account of Oneself)*, predatory power *(The Psychic Life of Power)*, melancholic subjectivity *(Precarious Life)*, and interpellation *(Excitable Speech)*. In her thought, bodily contingency drift is rendered fully, both in detail and definition.

Complexity

If the writings of Judith Butler can chronicle with such passionate eloquence the traces of the contingent body as it is simultaneously constituted by and, in turn, working through its often painful history of repression, disavowals, and exclusions, the perspective of Katherine Hayles does just the opposite. Refusing the language of psychoanalysis in favor of the new science(s) of information theory, privileging complexity theory over hauntology, the conflict between simulation and materiality in the regime of computation over problematics involved in performing gender, Hayles' thought captures the trajectory of body drift as it becomes fully entangled with its technological condition. It is not so much that Hayles is disinterested in questions of sexual difference, gender constitution, and queering bodies as that her thought is framed by its own hauntology, namely, her increasingly urgent understanding that the history of the human as we have traditionally understood the term, not only its social imperatives and political power but also its disavowals, exclusions, and repressions, has been overwhelmed by the sudden coming to be of a fundamental shift in the order of things, specifically, the appearance of the "regime of computation" as the dominant principle in a new house of (cyber-human) being. Refusing either to blissfully celebrate the digitizing of human experience within the soft skin of code-works or to lament the passing from history of the human as the ascendant species-form, Hayles pursues a very different strategy. In her thought, the regime of computation is chronicled with such philosophical passion, literary creativity, and scientific precision precisely because Hayles has grasped deeply and immediately the *political* significance of code studies, specifically, that the arrival of posthuman subjectivity is accompanied by the complex arrival of all other things beyond the "post-": postgender, postsexuality, postidentity, and postconsciousness. A champion of neither violent apocalypse nor quiet capitulation, Hayles suggests the possibility of a new humanism developed directly at the borderline of simulation and materiality. In her perspective, the scientific language of complexity theory—dissipative structures, fluidities, porous boundaries, and bifurcations—is projected beyond the boundaries of scientific debate to become the constitutive principles of a form of humanism enabled by the regime of computation. Here the grammar of the body is shifted from exclusive concern with questions of sexual normativity and gendered identity to a creative interrogation of what happens to questions of consciousness, sexuality, power, and culture in a computational culture in which the code moves aggressively from the visible to the invisible, from a history of prosthetics external to the body to a language of simulation fully internal to identity formation.

Indeed, in an important trilogy of books—*Writing Machines, How We Became Posthuman,* and *My Mother Was a Computer*[6]—Hayles elevated her concern with the unfolding development of cybernetic culture from a purely literary concern with digital humanities to a larger, and more intense, focus on the question of embodied consciousness in an age when information lost its body. Drawing the hard lesson from her interpretive history of cybernetics that the triumph of computational culture had introduced a worldview in which information was conceived as increasingly disembodied and immaterial, Hayles' project became that of introducing embodiment back into the picture and, with it, the question of subjectivity itself:

> I was interested in how we could put embodiment back into the picture while not neglecting the effect on subjectivities of this disembodied notion of information. And having explored that in *How We Became Posthuman,* it then seemed to me that I should take these lessons onto my home ground of literary studies and talk about texts as embodied entities, and that led to the second book in the trilogy, *Writing Machines,* where I was developing the idea of media-specific analysis, analysis that would be attentive to the material mode in which the texts were instantiated. And since computation is looming larger and larger in our contemporary world, the third book, *My Mother Was a Computer,* was then an attempt to extend these ideas into both a theoretical and interpretive practice that would talk about intermediation as the interaction of language and code, of print and electronic textuality, and analog and digital modes of transmission.[7]

For Hayles, complexity theory is bound up with these ideas "because complexity is about multi-agent, multi-causal situations which, of course, describes all of the social world and much of the biological world as well."[8] When the regime of computation, with its operating language of simulation models, replaces the signifying regimes of normativity, when the inherent complexity of recursive, "multi-agent, multi-causal situations" substitutes itself for the contingent language of disavowals, exclusions, and hauntology, then what is suddenly put at stake are received understandings of the liberal human subject. Hayles is explicit about this:

> Historically the idea of the liberal humanist subject which was accompanied by notions of free will, autonomy, rationality, consciousness as the seed of identity, and so forth, was deeply bound up with causal explanations in science. It was a science that was equipped to deal with a world in which there were weak or negligible interactions between different bodies, particles, etc. And so you can see how that notion translates into the idea of an autonomous self, possessed of rationality and free will. Those ideas, those paradigms, grew up together, they mutually reinforced each other and as much as those scientific ideas contributed to knowledge and technology and so forth, their weak point was always not being able to deal very effectively with complex systems. . . . So I think that these ideas of how the dynamics of complex systems work are applicable not only to explain social systems and the natural world, but also different disciplinary formations, like in my case literature and scientific fields as well. It's distributed, it relies on a whole infrastructure of extended cognition, it is multi-causal and intensely recursive.[9]

A visionary of the digital future, Hayles refuses received interpretations of the liberal human subject in favor of drawing the truly radical lessons to be learned from the regime of computation. Here the body of the future is enabled by distributed consciousness; augmented by extended cognition; circulated through fast-moving, recursive loops of information; always caught up in multicausal, multiagent networks of information; and all the while never constrained by the causal but motivated by recombinant possibilities. When the "idea of the liberal human subject" is undermined by the recursive loops of complexity theory, when code replaces logos, serious implications follow for understanding the body in society. Not only are the politics of the body suddenly interpolated by the language of software as ideology but also, in Hayles' perspective, the traditional relationship of human subjectivity to technology undergoes a historic, perhaps cosmological, revision. Rejecting the perspective of technological determinism as much as the celebration of technology as a (religious) singularity, Hayles' cultural achievement lies in suggesting a critical perspective on technology, in which the human species limits itself to that of a "co-evolving" partner in the relationship, and, against the technical will to disembodiment and immateriality, that human subjectivity recover the possibility of embodied consciousness. Everything in Hayles' writings anticipates depth participation by the body in the question of technology. Forgoing a perspective on technology in society in which technicity remains external to the body, Hayles explores the multiple ways by which the body has been effectively territorialized by the regime of computation. An intellectual pilgrim exploring the digital future, her writings are present at the transformation of the body literally into a writing machine, simultaneously a writer of code by also inscribing in its deepest interiority the language of code. In her writings, technological humanism finally finds its theoretical voice. Abjuring a form of thought that remains purely exterior to the object of its attention, Hayles writes out in text after text the multiplicity of bodies—scientific, literary, aesthetic, practical—that we have become in the age of distributed consciousness and extended cognition. Aligning her thought with the latest developments in neuroscience as the cultural zeitgeist of the digital age, Hayles chronicles the tentative, yet irresistible, emergence of the body wearing the skin of computation. Finding her "tutor texts" wherever she can, her writings trace the regulatory codes of the soft skin body from its first discovery in the history of computer science proper to its later appearances in literary fiction and digital textuality and, finally, to its most recent, recursive iterations in mobility and augmentation. More than is customary for a theorist of the digital humanities, Hayles' thought runs alongside the great cultural discoveries of the twentieth-first century. And well it might, for what is really at stake in her theorizations is less a prolegomenon to a new paradigm of digital humanities—although that, too—and more the emergence of a form of thought that has successfully captured the very first glimmerings of the unfolding, yet unknowable, destiny of the deeply coded, deeply embodied multicausal, multiagent bodies that we increasingly inhabit in the regime of computation. A feminist of distributed consciousness, a scientist of the body recursive, a designer of writing machines, a poet of code studies, Hayles can recommend so insistently, and enthusiastically, the methodological strategy of "intermediations" because that is what her intellectual comportment represents in the end: an intensive, layered, recursive intermediation of the very best of the creative human imagination with the stubborn facts of a regime of computation still in the process of emerging into the light-time and light-space of society.

Hybridity

If Judith Butler destabilizes both feminism and queer theory by problematizing gendered sexuality, on one hand, and the shifting boundaries of lesbian and gay sexuality, on the other, in favor of a critical exploration of the necessarily fluid yet materially situated space of alternative forms of sexuality—transgendered, transsexual, and intersex—Donna Haraway goes one step further. Motivated by the same spirit of patient, critical deconstruction but aiming at the sexual inscriptions and gendered identities imposed by the "informatics of domination," Haraway undermines her earlier self, the cybernetic self of her famous essay "The Cyborg Manifesto." Whatever the reason—the slow passage of time, the immediate pressure of political events, her attunement to the field of genetic biology, or simply a deep desire on her part to rethink the foundational logic of animals, humans, plants, and minerals—this Haraway, the Haraway of such important books as *Primate Visions, The Companion Species Manifesto,* and *Simians, Cyborgs, and Women*—cannot, and most certainly does not, think any longer in binary terms. She has even fled the comfortable feminist space of preferring "to be a cyborg than a goddess."[10] Now she would prefer to be a "companion species"—to understand other evocative forms of communication between animals and humans. And she does not stop there but has actually written out in words the textual pleasures of a hybrid language—creative essays that are populated with asides, memories, scientific theory, political critique, part autobiography, part eloquent conceptualization. It is not only a woman's theory, although that, too—knotted, messy, uncomfortable, full of pauses and replacements and sudden surprising juxtapositions of meaning—but something else, truly hybrid writing that honors a form of theorizing the body and that has hybridity as both its privileged object of attention and its aesthetic style.

While the thought of Katherine Hayles delivers us to a world populated with a new appearance of being—data flesh—Haraway's concept of hybridity is different. In a way that can only be fictionally suggested by the double personality of Katherine and Kate in *Writing Machines,* the hybrid body only knows the borderlines, the intersections, the ruptures, the unsituated. This is the case for a specific reason. Neither pure information nor pure flesh, the hybrid body knots the strange experience of being digital, being plant, being animal, being mineral into a beautiful labyrinth of knowledge. Refusing to stay at the borderline of literature and science or, for that matter, of biology and feminism, Haraway explores different forms of life that appear when the borderline comes inside our bodies and *we* become the intersections, ruptures, and intermediations of our most creative imagination. All this to say that while Haraway's hybrid body has much in common politically with Butler's courageous resistance to the demands of heterosexual normative intelligibility and definitely shares the same sense of complexity that winds through Hayles' complex bodies, it rises beyond both complexity and contingency to become their common borderline—not a borderline conceived as a permanent line of division but as a beautifully tangled knot where profound issues raised by Butler and Hayles, from bodies that matter to mothering computers, from regimes of sexual signification to regimes of computation, finally find ways of intermingling, intermediating, and perhaps even beginning the always difficult task of working through their differences. If that is the case, this would indicate that the thought of Donna Haraway, and with it the hybrid body, may well constitute the supplement, the difference, the margin to the two poles of the contingent body and the body of complexity.

The back legend to all of Haraway's thought is the notion that today more than ever, we no longer inhabit, if we ever have, a solitary body of flesh and bone but are ourselves the intersection of a multiplicity of bodies, with life itself as a fluid intersection of humans and plants and animals and minerals. Of course, from Haraway's perspective, perish the thought that such intersections will inevitably result in romantic naturalism. To study what she has to say about powerful parallels among barbaric practices directed against primates, racial violence directed against the black diaspora, and abuse of women suggests that Haraway privileges the intersection, the knot, the intermediation, not as utopian imaginaries but as ways of deepening her epic story of domination. It is the same situation when Haraway transitions her perspective on the science of the cyborg to the politics involved in the informatics of domination. While others might conclude their studies of the very same history of technology with more utopian aspirations for "being digital," Haraway proceeds to deepen the intersection of digital technology and laboring (women's) bodies into a grisly scenario involved with the informatics of domination as the newest, recursive loop in hypercapitalist globalization.

What Hayles suggests by paying attention to the scientific language of information theory, with its fractals and recursive loops, Haraway actually practices by way of a counterscience that attends closely to knots of exclusion, tangled semiotic webs of disavowal, and disappeared intermediations. Here the scientific language of information theory meets the recalcitrant hard matter of individual life histories, material social formations, and power alignments. What results is a vision of the hybrid body that captures so comprehensively and meticulously the future adventures and often tragic histories of the multiplicity of the bodies that we inhabit precisely because it resurfaces once again a forgotten form of thought, namely, the mythopoetic discourse surrounding the four humors—Earth, Air, Fire, Water. Haraway actually has written a book or a significant essay specializing in each of the four humors: Earth is *Primate Visions,* with its entangled story of biology, paleoanthropology, and rich material histories of racism; Air is the brilliant light-stream of thought that is "The Cyborg Manifesto"; Fire is the implosive, intellectual energy of *Simians, Cyborgs, and Women,* with its profound intersectional themes tracing a hegemonic history of cultural domination across the gender, the species, and the machines; and finally, Water is the liquid imagination of *Companion Species,* with its circulatory flows of evocative communication among the coevolving partnership of animals and humans. Equally, in the ancient spirit of discourse, the four humors, which never were considered in isolation from one another but rather as deeply inflected, deeply complementary dimensions of the body, nature, and life itself, all of Haraway's writings represent an eloquent attempt to begin again the conversation of Earth, Air, Fire, and Water—except this time with the addition of the distinctly new element involved with the emergence of the informatics of domination, to reconfigure the myth of the four humors to include spaces of indeterminacy, uncertainty, and unsituated hybridities. When biology itself is blasted away by technologies moving at the speed of light; when paleoanthropology is forced to accommodate power speaking in the name of neuroscience;

when companion species sometimes stumble over the bedrock of fixed genders, sexual stereotyping, and (human) species hubris; the discourse of the four humors must admit a small, but relevant, revision in the direction of Speed-Earth, Speed-Air, Speed-Fire, and Speed-Water.

If the multiplicity of bodies that we are now inhabit a world of hyper-humors, if even the most ancient understandings of the elementary matter of life have been fully penetrated by technologies of globalization and their powerful ideologies supporting heterosexual normativity, hierarchy of species, and disciplinary knowledge, it follows that we are in desperate need of a new way of being multiple, hybrid, and bodily. The singularity of Donna Haraway finds its most intense expression in the fact that producing such an imaginative reconsideration of new relations among species, bodies, and power is exactly what has gained her writing such immense purchase on contemporary intellectuality. And of course, in the way of all things historically understood, the earliest intimation of profound changes in future cultural constructions is most often found in those creative knots of thought, those brilliant intermediations, in this case, of the possibility of the hybrid body that is the intellectual legacy of Donna Haraway. Returning to the discourse of biology from which her thought originally emerged, Haraway's vision of the hybrid body is a theoretical genome intermediating past and future, an idea so germane, so suitable for its recombinant times, that it already exists as the *unconscious knowledge* of the future—not simply anticipatory, as in the case of preconsciousness, or fully aware, like consciousness itself, but resolutely the unconscious knowledge that will most certainly be carried by words, bodies, struggles, strange intersections, yet unknowable circumstances from past and present to the future. Like a shaman at the meeting of earthly racism, liquid technologies of power, digital clouds, and political fires, Haraway's thought, unconsciously but no less decisively, has reconciled the contingent and the complex into a vision of the hybridity that we are fated to become in this future-land of the present.

Theory Drift: Visions of the Posthuman Future

To study the thought of Butler, Hayles, and Haraway is to be sud-denly caught up in a space and time of incommensurability, shad-owed by the thought of those who have come before and yet open to new histories emergent. Definitely refusing to remain inscribed within the boundaries of canonical knowledge, they have had the intellectual courage to absorb fully into their thought the repressed instincts of melancholic culture, the nihilism of world alienation, and the profound social transformations produced by the triumph of the regime of computation. As singular representatives of a form of thought that is fully alert to its historical times, the texts of Butler, Hayles, and Haraway permit meditative entrance directly into the great crises of contemporary society, politics, and culture. Butler takes us to the edge of rethinking the boundaries of the human in a time of perpetual war; Hayles turns herself into a parodic "writ-ing machine" to find a dwelling place for the creative imagination within the austere landscape of the culture of code; and Haraway is the one contemporary thinker to have begun the necessary ethical project of working through a new language of possible reconcili-ation among previously warring species.

And yet for all this, if their thought can be so brilliantly reso-nant of the primary crises of these posthuman times, it is probably because each of their intellectual projects bears the discernible traces of that which has come before. Indeed, in terms of my own intellectual autobiography, I began reflecting on Butler, Hayles, and Haraway after a sustained intellectual journey through the writings of Heidegger, Marx, and Nietzsche. Intent on understanding the pathways of the will as it has moved from its modern expression as a will to power to its posthuman appearance as a will to technology, I was struck by how powerfully the thought of Butler, Hayles, and Haraway completed the still unanswered, still enigmatic pleas for understanding and practice immanent to the texts of Heidegger, Marx, and Nietzsche. Not that there is any necessary logically reductive correspondence between these two sets of thinkers, but there is one thing they hold in common, namely, a passionate intensity about registering in words not only what is avowed, coded, animated by the power of the will but also what remains marginalized, silenced, disappeared by the drift of histories that, taken in part or in whole, constitute the posthuman future. While Heidegger, Marx, and Nietzsche may have first anticipated a *human* future that would soon be dominated by the will to technology, it is my sense that it is the specific contribution of Butler, Hayles, and Haraway to have identified body drift as the fateful talisman to the *posthuman* future. In their writings, it is as if the great narratives of theoretical critique—power, sex, gender, species-logic, race, code—have been suddenly set adrift, dispersed, and yet for all that, wonderfully intermediated, entangled, and worked through. The enigma remains, of course, whether the will to technology and body drift are key circuits in a common pattern of political history that quickly ascends through the scale of domination or whether the emergence of body drift as the sign of the posthuman par excellence is only the inception of something fundamentally new, something lying in anxious balance between politically orchestrated cataclysm and an always unlegislated, unanticipated insurgence by bodies that have never mattered, never counted, never coded.

Whatever the case, mindful of the past, dissatisfied with the present, and visionary about the future, critical feminism defines in advance three major vectors of a posthuman future yet to be realized. Here the *postmodernism* of Judith Butler, the *posthumanism* of Katherine Hayles, and the *companionism* of Donna Haraway represent possible pathways to the posthuman future—pathways that both follow a logic of descent into the complexities of contemporary history and yet draw into presence a posthuman future still in the process of revealing itself. Always an uneasy convergence of opposing tendencies—received material histories of the body deeply marked by questions of class, race, and gender versus a future of increasingly virtualized body experiences—the posthuman future is fully present in the tradition of critical feminism. For example, despite all the enthusiastic extropian visions of technologically ablated bodies driven to feverish moments of technological singularity, it is abundantly clear that the future politics of the body will continue to be contested on the familiar grounds of class, race, and gender. Indeed, it might even be said that the real impact of global technologies of communication has not been so much to realize a much-hoped-for utopia of communicative communitariansm as to expose the enduring political appeal of the most recidivist and violent traditions of sexual violence, gender apartheid, and class inequalities. In such a circumstance, Butler's singular focus on processes of "critical desubjectivication" as possible antidotes to a "passionate attachment to subjection" provides very necessary political guidance to the uncertain future of the posthuman body. Equally, Butler's reflections on the continuing ethical appeal of Antigone are all the more remarkable for their powerful anticipation of a present political history instantly distinguishable by the resurgence of political tyranny, from the new security state so integrated into the political logic of the West to the fundamental struggle between freedom and authoritarianism that is the mark of all the Arab Springs of contemporary politics. While it is still not clear what will ultimately emerge from the crossing of the posthuman syntagm, one thing is fully evident: the future history of the body will surely bear the mark of postmodern signifying processes as much as it will have its subjectivity constituted by regimes of computation. Whether the tension of living at the edge of postmodern signification and posthuman virtualities will ultimately produce forms of subjectivity receptive to the inspiring language of companion species remains to be seen. And yet, for all the indeterminacy of the future, there is no avoiding the conclusion that the multiple bodies that we inhabit are continuing pilgrimages across the landscape of postmodernism, posthumanism, and companionism.

Indeed, Butler, Hayles, and Haraway can so powerfully anticipate the most important tendencies of contemporary society

because their writings do not appear in isolation but rather comple-
ment and expand on a powerful tradition of critique elucidated in
all its complexity by the different visions proffered by Heidegger,
Marx, and Nietzsche. In this case, Butler can interpret Nietzsche's
On the Genealogy of Morals with such brilliance because her writing in effect "overcomes" Nietzsche's understanding of prosthetic
subjectivity. In Butler's writings, Nietzsche's genealogy of liberal
subjectivity, simultaneously constituted by regimes of political
intelligibility and fully reactive in its dominant psychological formations, is completed in a way that fully bears the traces of its own
hauntologies, disavowals, and exclusions. Equally, while Heidegger
privileged an always unreconciled tension between *technē* and
poiēsis as the essence of the language of technology, Hayles "overcomes" Heidegger by refusing to accept the terms of the binary
at the heart of identity and difference, namely, by bringing to the
surface of critical consciousness ways of working through the ethics
of the complex, the bifurcated, the fractured, the incommensurable.
It is the very same with Donna Haraway, whose thought might have
begun with a powerful description of the informatics of domination
as the essence of the digital commodity-form but whose lasting
importance is to have introduced anew those other knots of understanding made possible by the complex hybridities and entangled
life-forms of a world composed of companion species. Whereas
Marx may have rehearsed in his theoretical imagination the once
and future material history associated with the historical triumph of
capitalist political economy, it remains the particular contribution
of Donna Haraway to have articulated a chilling description of the
ruins of Marx's "dead labor" in the language of the informatics of
domination, while simultaneously advancing beyond Marx in her
critical vision of contemporary capitalism, namely, that capitalism
in the age of information culture has given rise to truly predatory
forms of earth-alienation that can only be effectively resisted by
ethically reconciling humans with their biomaterial companions.

Taken together, the writings of Butler, Hayles, and Haraway

constitute the leading exemplars of a new tradition of critical feminism that is all the more intellectually compelling and politically insightful because it stands perfectly poised between past and future, between, that is, its theoretical dialogue with the dark prophets of modernity—Heidegger, Marx, and Nietzsche—and its insistence that the future be thought anew in the language of the contingent, the complex, and the hybrid. In this sense, critical feminism is important not only for the content of its theoretical analysis but as a *form* of thought that captures eloquently and succinctly the key trajectories of the posthuman future. In effect, if the posthuman future promises to be fractured, bifurcated, uncertain, then why not a form of thought that is equal to its posthistorical times, one that understands from within the politics of contingency, the ethics of complexity, and the ontology of the hybrid by translating body drift into a language privileging the relational, the complicated, the partial?

Indeed, if the modern century began with the premonitory visions of Nietzsche, Heidegger, and Marx, who, in the strikingly different languages of aphorism, metaphysics, and insurgency, anticipated the greater historical current of the will to technology, that century truly finds both its eclipse and its transcendence in the equally prophetic visions of Butler, Hayles, and Haraway. In this case, early intimations of body drift as a central feature of contemporary social experience are to be found in the thought of Nietzsche, Heidegger, and Marx.[11] After all, what haunts Marx's critique of political economy is its truly ominous vision of the desiccated bodies of capitalist society: bodies that circulate in the language of exchange-value, inscribed by all the empty signs of political economy, valorized by the predatory logic of the commodity-form, and coded by the regime of capital accumulation. If Marx prophesied bodies fetishized by the commodity-form, continuously mobilized and interpellated by all the signs of propertied accumulation, Heidegger went one step further by throwing off the language of political economy in favor of a radical deconstruction of the metaphysics of modernity. For Heidegger, the pleasure of subjugation as the constitutive ontology of contemporary subjectivity is based on the fact that production of bodily experience during the contemporary epistēmē is fully entangled in the powerful current of an emergent technological experience. Here body drift is distinguished by an increasingly technical language of ordering, coded as "standing-reserve," with bodies always maintained in readiness for instant mobilization, reduced to an ethics of "abuse value" and invested by a social psyche marked by the "malice of strife." With Nietzsche, this gathering current of thought concerning the fate of the body in the modern century finds its philosophical capstone. Here bodies are born in *ressentiment,* taking pleasure in making of themselves "conscience vivisectionists," transforming bad conscience over their own repressed instincts onto convenient social scapegoats, projecting an aura of slave consciousness toward ruling ascetic priests while all the while assenting to capricious violence against the weak, the powerless, the excluded.

What distinguishes the critical feminism of Butler, Hayles, and Haraway, making of their thought something simultaneously retrospective and projective, is that their inquiries effectively represent the late-twentieth- and early-twenty-first-century counterparts of a tradition of thought formulated in all its passionate intensity and unanswerable enigmas by Marx, Heidegger, and Nietzsche—certainly not in a reductive or reiterative sense, but in the larger meaning of critical intellectual imagination, namely, that in this renewed tradition of critical feminism, the fate of the body first theorized in the differing vocabularies of historical materialism, nihilism, and bad conscience is taken up once more. Literally, the thought of Butler, Hayles, and Haraway begins in the wasteland of modernity, that point where the cultural ravages anticipated by Marx's dead labor, Heidegger's completed nihilism, and Nietzsche's bad conscience finds its most intensified, indeed globalized, experience. What makes the thought of critical feminism truly original and, indeed, of urgent importance is that while Butler, Hayles, and Haraway fully absorb the dark legacy of their philosophical predecessors, they commonly insist on renewing the gamble of intellectual critique. Not only does their thought, individually and collectively, intensify the gathering darkness by showing in multiple registers—gender, sexuality, primates, computation—the changed order of being that is postmodern, posthuman, and postspecies experience but, in some essential respects, it effectively overturns the political economy of Marx, the metaphysical critique of Heidegger, and the philosophy of Nietzsche.

For example, in Butler's thought, the philosophical passion that is Nietzsche—the Nietzsche of the end of history, the end of subjectivity, the end of time, the end of power—finds its moment of completion and renewal. Strikingly postmodern in her reflections, Butler is one with Nietzsche in understanding that power is always a doubled sign, constituted as much by its psychic affirmations as by its necessary disavowals, exclusions, and absences. Indeed, if Butler can stipulate that the ontological formation of subjectivity is inherently "tropological," that is only to reiterate the earlier insight of Nietzsche that power is always a cynical sign, a "perspectival simulacra" that can be so seductive precisely because it is the enduring object of what Butler aptly describes as our "passionate attachment to subjection." In Butler's writings, the postmodern vision that is Nietzsche, this vision of power at the edge of discipline and seduction, finds its most faithful social historian and its most critical undermining. If Butler can write out the contemporary politics of *Precarious Life,* if she can interpret *Antigone's Choice* as the horizon of public ethics today, if she can express so eloquently the forgotten histories of bodies that don't matter in a time of militarism, sacrificial violence, and economic pestilence, that is because Butler has done that which Nietzsche intimated but never fulfilled, namely, she has descended into the logic of signification to discover its perils and possibilities. In this sense, Butler is actually Nietzsche turning back on himself, that point where the logic of the sign, the signs of gender, sexuality, kinship, and power, seeks out that which has been disavowed, disappropriated, disowned as the once and certain talisman of new hauntologies of the posthuman—this time, though, not hauntologies in the form of a fatal curse but posthuman hauntologies that insist that the bodily memories of the disenfranchised, the dehumanized, the disavowed be translated anew into an inspiring language of political contingency.

In a similar way, if Hayles privileges an exploration of the regime of computation as opposed to Butler's interest in regimes of social intelligibility, that is because Hayles' interest lies not with the signs of the postmodern but with the codes of the posthuman. What is noteworthy about Hayles is that in her work, she explores the full consequences of Heidegger's question of technology. While Heidegger might have claimed that the rising technological reality would be based on a logic of enframing in which processes of technological ordering would be primary, it was left to Katherine Hayles to note that the passage to the posthuman would take place primarily through the ordering logic of the regime of computation. Equally, while Heidegger emphasized the reduction of being in the age of technology to a "standing-reserve" oscillating between boredom and abuse value, he always held to the doubled ethical possibility of technological nihilism, namely, that the greater the danger, the greater the prospect of building, dwelling, thinking. In this sense, Hayles completes Heidegger by taking him at his word, balancing her description of the regime of computation with a special fascination for "tutor texts" that are invariably disruptive, bifurcated, paradoxical, complex. While Heidegger may have cautioned in his "Letter on Humanism" that "homelessness is coming to be the destiny of the world,"[12] he also noted that in the face of the gathering storm of homelessness, we must "first learn to exist in the nameless." That, I believe, is the special intellectual vocation of Katherine Hayles. Noteworthy for her fascination with the pleasure of the (scientific) text, indeed driven by a rigorous literary commitment to faithfully record the enframing logic of the power of the code, Hayles makes of each of her texts an exercise in learning how "to exist in the nameless." In her thought, what Baudrillard once described as the "terrorism of the code" is effectively countered by an electronic poetics of disruption—technical order is complicated by digital chaos—with the result that complexity itself is revealed to be a way of existing in the nameless.

Curiously, for a thinker whose famous earlier aspiration to be a "cyborg rather than a goddess" has been undermined in favor of being a companion species, Donna Haraway is the one thinker who has not only truly understood Marx's vision of dead labor but has turned her thought into a sustained exercise in dwelling on the fatal implications of such a dark prophecy. Avowedly a materialist historian, an exponent of a form of bioscientific imagination that remains faithful to the traditional injunction for truth-saying, a thinker who dwells at the borderlines of the primate, the human, the semiotic, the environment, the lasting contribution of Haraway is to have grasped the essential insight that something resembling Marx's dead labor, or what Hannah Arendt once described as "earth alienation," is the core logic animating the contemporary techno-logical epistēmē. Always a critical feminist, Haraway's response to the gathering darkness has been neither to take refuge in a form of political economy that merely recapitulates the technological logic of the modern nor to subordinate her thought to a liberal project of environmental sustainability that serves to reinforce existent pat-terns of class inequalities and unjust power distributions but rather to do something truly radical and, in that radicality, truly original. The first and best of all the theorists of hybridity, Haraway's project has been to make of the incommensurable, the incompossible, the disavowed, the excluded, the center point of a new metaphysics of experience—certainly not a metaphysics of exclusively human experience, but something hybrid, bio-material-semiotic-human experience, a metaphysics of the unreconciled, the fractured border, the liquid membrane. In Haraway's thought, there is rehearsed for the first time a way of thinking, and potentially acting, that reflects on the implications of a future of dead labor, dead culture, dead power, dead species, and dead environments with intellectual intensity, political sincerity, and inspiring theoretical originality. In this new way of thinking, a pathway through and beyond a present of negative being finally makes its appearance, at first tentatively and only faintly, but later with growing confidence in the power of its theoretical analysis, namely, that the future belongs to those dwelling at the borderlines, to those who make of their bio-social-ecological abode the hybrid, the intermediation, the splice.

2

CONTINGENCIES: NIETZSCHE IN DRAG IN THE THEATER OF JUDITH BUTLER

Perhaps most importantly, we must recognize that ethics requires us to risk ourselves precisely at moments of unknowingness, when what forms us diverges from what lies before us, when our willingness to become undone in relation to others constitutes our chance of becoming human.

—Judith Butler, *Giving an Account of Oneself*

After Antigone

Could there be any text more appropriate to both understanding and perhaps, if the winds of fate are favorable, *transforming* contemporary politics than Judith Butler's eloquent study of moral philosophy, *Giving an Account of Oneself*?

Resisting the most powerful political currents of the times, breaking decisively with the regulatory regime of normativity, speaking eloquently, passionately, historically about another ethics, another body, another space, Butler injects into contemporary public debate something that was thought to have been lost forever: what she herself once described as the "shameless impurity" of Antigone—not Antigone as a haunting figure of the eternal struggle between state and kinship but that other Antigone, the forgotten Antigone of the burial chamber, who, in the end, preferred death to irresponsibility, the unrequited passion of love to self-preservation. It is this Antigone, this *ethical* remembrance of Antigone, who, against all reasonable expectation, returns from her incarceration in the burial chamber to finally break her silence in *Giving an Account of Oneself*, to say finally what needs to be articulated, namely, that now as then, an "ethics of responsibility" may be the only measure of real kinship in a culture patterned by an "ethics of violence"—and to say this not dogmatically, not with the certainty of an abstract universal but in a rhetorical analysis which in its hesitations, nuances, and sudden transfigurations does honor to the equally forgotten language of contingency.

Because that is what *Giving an Account of Oneself* specifically, and Judith Butler's thought in general, is really about: it is simultaneously a plea for the return of that which is most frail, vulnerable, unintelligible, unknowable, unrepresentable in political thought and a lament for that which has been lost in the coming to be of the most recent of the real-world iterations of Hegel's vision of the "universal homogenous state." In this ethical demand for the recovery of the contingent in human affairs, being *human* is itself, in the first instance, that impossibility of interpellation by the codes of abstract universalism—simultaneously constituted by and authorizing power—while, at the same moment, dwelling in the borderlands of other equally contingent *social* beings, each with their own hauntology of unknowability, unintelligibility, and unrepresentability. Which is why Butler can argue so persuasively in undermining Žižek that the real has never been understandable exclusively in the language of lack—fear of castration, fear of the law—but only in the more complex terms of silent foreclosures and fatal contestations. More than is customary, the thought of Judith Butler is a continuing, insistent reiteration of, and rebellion against, the abyssal silence of an ethics that would be vulnerable, finite, and unintelligible in this time after Antigone, not only in the sense that Butler's writings always trace the phantasmal, yet tangible, presence of life and death in all the great signifiers, whether of kinship, gender, sexuality, or power, but for a different reason. Butler is truly after Antigone because her writings represent most directly and powerfully the haunting question left by Antigone, namely, what are the lasting claims of kinship, love, and fealty, that is to say, the claims of compassion and social solidarity, in a world suddenly divested of its reasons by the presence of evil.

Now, of course, the mark designated by the appellation—*After Antigone*—is the evil demon of all models of power that originate in Nietzsche's caesura. Nietzsche could reflect with such devastating insight in *Thus Spake Zarathustra* that the logic of the self-identical could never rest easy with the necessary contingency of "time's it was" precisely because the will to power would be based, then as it is now, on the death of death. Evacuating lived relationality from the moment of death—disavowing the fully contingent relation of our bodies to the cyclical wheel of time, the relation of bodies to the sacred, the profane, the mortal, and indeed to the "problem" of mortality itself—is the worm that turns in the post-Enlightenment mind and, before that, in the cosmologies of the Christian confessional, and most vividly in their full exposure to the light of antireason in all the genealogical texts of Nietzsche. But if the excommunication of knowledge of that which is most contingent, relational, intelligible, vulnerable from modern subjectivity is the mythological price exacted by the death of death, this also would suggest that the mark of death's singularity—our own—which has gone missing from the human story is fated to return as the specter that haunts human passions. Privilege the question of contingency and the narrative of all the master referents—power, gender, sexuality, knowledge, desire—immediately come unglued. Disavowal of the contingency of the human situation is the necessary gesture of a power, a body, a reason, a desire that would seek to substitute itself for the lost language of the gods who, in the face of this challenge, continue to maintain their long silence, hidden in shadows from human view.

But if we are not to passively mime the psychic strategy of disavowal nor lament the flight of the gods, we should, for all that, remain attentive to the sentiment of Antigone at work in *Giving an Account of Oneself*. Of Antigone herself, Judith Butler likes to repeat the beautiful refrain that she was always "between living and dying," a faithful—indeed, a *responsible*—sister and daughter whose loyalty to the honor of death in a land of evil made of her the first of all the posthumans, a postmoralist who recuperated the human by choosing the singularity of (her own) death. A "shameless impurity" certainly: remembering Antigone, recalling to mind the incommensurability of "between living and dying" is also to refuse the honor of the name of life of power, to add additional complexity to kinship based on blood. But more than that, the designation *After Antigone* calls to mind that those who would think the question of an "ethics of responsibility" in the imperial storm-center of an "ethics of violence" are also fated to represent a form of thought and practice which is itself beyond living and dying.

Antigone's Claim is, of course, the extended intellectual meditation that constitutes in all its philosophical intensity and social commitment the life of Judith Butler. A philosopher, political theorist, deconstructionist of all things gendered and bodied and spoken and written and performed, her intellectual comportment does honor to the name of Antigone. By her voice, variously analytical, poetic, theoretical, and always a rhetoric-machine, she returns the enigmatic fate of Antigone to public scrutiny—not only for a psychoanalytical practice that would finally turn from Oedipus to Antigone but for a political theory of the state, of the body, of desire in all its genders and sexes that would seek out the traces of intelligibility, of responsibility, of contingency in their living materiality. Someday, and why not this day perhaps, it may well be said of Butler what she once remarked about Antigone:

> She acts, she speaks, she becomes one for whom the speech act is a fatal crime, but this fatality exceeds her life and enters the discourse of intelligibility as its own promising fatality, the social forum of its aberrant, unprecedented future.[1]

All of Butler's speech acts are "fatal crimes" which only enter the discourse of intelligibility as their relentless overturning, the philosophical forum of its "aberrant, unprecedented future." A theorist of performance, performing *Gender Trouble,* performing *Bodies That Matter,* performing *Excitable Speech,* performing *Antigone's Claim,* performing *The Psychic Life of Power,* she is, for all of that, always seduced by her own undoing—not just *Undoing Gender,* the scandal of undoing power, undoing intelligibility, undoing violence, undoing representation, undoing Hegel, Freud, Foucault, Levinas, Žižek, and Agamben, and, of course, undoing Nietzsche most of all.

And why not? Judith Butler is Nietzsche in drag. Not the bitter Nietzsche with the bad conscience that he promptly circuited into the essays comprising *On the Genealogy of Morals* but that other spectral, imaginary Nietzsche, his double, who, until now, lurking in the shadows at the side of the stage of philosophy, finally makes his dancing entrance in the theater of Judith Butler in the drag outfit of the "transvaluation of values." As Butler shows with brilliant detail in *The Psychic Life of Power,* Nietzsche's thought always hovered around the stone that closed the burial chamber of "time's it was," listening intently to the intimations of human deprivation, the first and best witness to the upsurge of the "last man," the earliest prophet of the dark future of ressentiment, the philosopher who would note that this, the most consciously post-Christian of all eras, would be the most marked by the sign of the crucified Christ. While Nietzsche literally threw speech ahead of his dying body, writing posthumously about the "turn" in the circuit of power that signaled the beginning of something radically original—something constituted by power yet, at the same time, its "fatal crime"—namely, the "transvaluation of values," he was by temperament unsuited to the task of illuminating the "dancing star" of this "unprecedented future." Bad conscience never escapes the mythological riddles of unhappy consciousness. In essence, bad conscience preserves while always disavowing its basis in unhappy consciousness.

Contingent Power

But not Butler. She begins precisely where Nietzsche left off. That's the emotional capstone of *The Psychic Life of Power*. Certainly this text is an eloquent meditation on Hegel's unhappy consciousness, Nietzsche's bad conscience, Freud's melancholic ego, Foucault's normalizing power, and Althusser's concept of interpellation, but its deepest connecting thread is the stubborn, recalcitrant thought of Nietzsche—and not just any Nietzsche, but the "less than human" Nietzsche of *On the Genealogy of Morals*: the Nietzsche whose mind thinks its way into the galactic debris field left by the implosion of two thousand years of Christian metaphysics and the rising star, dim at first but then quickly burning luminescent, of the bourgeois ego. *This* Nietzsche is present everywhere in Butler's thought, certainly not always openly, but in the more subtle, and consequently pervasive, sense that Butler reading Nietzsche is, in effect, *Nietzsche undoing Butler*; that her thought is, in the best sense, undermined by the crucial insight that Nietzsche expressed in *On the Genealogy of Morals* concerning the appearance of a *purely perspectival will*—a "concept-fiction"—which, animated by bad conscience, turns back on itself, and on account of which modern subjectivity is doomed to be forever trapped in the logical circuitry—the "sorry bind"—of its own figuration and ground.

It has been remarked often enough that Butler is a Hegelian, her thought framed by the metaphysics of *The Phenomenology of Spirit*, by, that is, the challenge of articulating a form of thought that takes account of the dialectic of inclusion and exclusion while simultaneously effectively undermining this (epistemological) mirror of the self-identical. But Butler's purported subordination to Hegelian dialectics does not take into consideration that the passion of Nietzsche has itself effectively supplanted the world-spirit of reason. Like the classical tradition of Greek idealism before him, Hegel attempted to solve the historical riddle of the broken field of mind and body by appealing to the unifying capacities of the will to reason. That the Hegelian resolution of the problem of the divided will could not be resolved by a flight from human vicissitudes to the (self-identical) will to reason was signaled by those competing (political) futures in the *Phenomenology*: the fable of "Lordship and Bondage" as the foundational text of the critique of political economy and "Unhappy Consciousness" as the premonitory shadow cast sixty years in advance of Nietzsche's essays in the *Genealogy*. Perhaps herself a "less than human" Hegelian, a theorist who honors the name of Hegel by listening attentively to the clues to our shared historical destiny hidden in the textual interstices of the *Phenomenology,* Butler's instinct has always been to search for the Nietzsche in Hegel, tracing the "terror of the body" in all its violence from the pages of *On the Genealogy of Morals* to its original appearance in *The Phenomenology of Spirit*:

> Here, consciousness in its full abjection has become like shit, lost in a self-referential anality, a circle of its own making. In Hegel's words, "we have here a personality confined to its own self and its petty actions, a personality brooding over itself, as wretched as it is impoverished."[2]

This is Butler's excremental Hegel—not the unfolding of the world-spirit of reason nor the "self-referential" dialectic of reason but something more "abject," motivated by "negative narcissism," fully preoccupied with "what is most debased and defiled" about itself: in short, Hegel's "unhappy consciousness."

> Regarding itself as a nothing, as a doing of nothing, as an excremental function, and hence regarding itself as excrement, this consciousness effectively reduces itself to the changeable features of its bodily functions and features. Yet, since it is an experience of wretchedness, there is some consciousness which takes stock of these functions and which is not fully identified with them. Significantly, it is here, in the effort to differentiate

itself from its excretory functions, indeed, from its excretory identity that consciousness relies on a mediator that Hegel calls a "priest." This mediating agency relieves the abject consciousness of responsibility for its own actions.[3]

When self-negation becomes a body invader and "unhappy consciousness" invests itself fully in the future of its bodily functions, we are in the presence of a powerful current of thought migrating inexorably from the remains of *The Phenomenology* to the future that is the *Genealogy,* from Hegel's broken dreams to Nietzsche's bad conscience. That the Hegelian resolution of the world-crisis of the divided will—the fatal splitting of mind and body, in short, "abject consciousness"—could not be achieved by an appeal to the unifying capacities of selfsame reason was rehearsed long before Hegel by the earlier futilities of Greek enlightenment. "Born posthumously," without (idealist) faith-based illusions in the "unchangeable" and the "immanent," Nietzsche knew better. The first and best of all contingent thinkers, he made of his thought a circuit through which all of the abjections, disavowals, and negations of two thousand years of Christian experiments aimed at resolving the crisis of divided consciousness would be projected onto that vulnerable, frail, resentment-driven, yet for all that dreamer of the vanished gods we call the contingent histories of the (human) body. While Butler provides in *The Psychic Life of Power* a dense knot of psychoanalytical reasons for her recovery of the Nietzsche in Hegel, there is always in the text a sense of something not yet named, still not recuperated, not said, something "perspectival," a "concept-fiction" put in play by Nietzsche. Because isn't that what the "psychic life of power" really is—a "concept-fiction," a purely *perspectival* reality that generates the concept of the body, gender, consciousness, identity, and, most of all, the abject self as ways of simultaneously drawing into presence and hiding from view the delirious nothingness, what Hannah Arendt described as the "negative will" of the modern project?

When Butler brushes the *Genealogy* against *The Phenomenology*, it is as if an astral gateway opens, out of which rushes all the Nietzsche in Butler. All the "concept-fictions" are there in all their primal violence: Nietzsche's "ascetic priests" return as the policing of "compulsory heterosexuality": the concept of ressentiment forms the psychogeography of Butler's critique of the culture of injury; Hegel's unhappy consciousness is revealed to be the ethical reflex of Nietzsche's bad conscience; everywhere "there is no formation of the subject without a passionate attachment to subjection";[4] the will "turns back" on itself; the (gendered) body "turns back" on itself; conscience "turns back" on itself; and everywhere Butler's overall political project—reoccupying the site of injury as the only way of working through possibilities for transformation, transfiguration, fabrication—has its origins as a compelling counterchallenge to Nietzsche's "ascetic priests," who only open the wound (of ressentiment) to stir up "chestnuts" of injured grievance.

And why not? More a theorist of the play of powers and dominations in cultural politics than a writer of intellectual history, Butler's teasing out of the Nietzsche in Hegel resonates with the contemporary public scene. The political culture that implicitly contextualizes all her work is that of the United States, the dynamic, planetary spearhead of the fully realized "universal homogenous state." Technologically accelerating at the speed of light, social reality is itself now in the process of being consumed by the paradoxes of light-time and light-space, and *light-power*. Social history is now perhaps best understood in the language of astrophysics, which implies that a culture moving at light-speed is not exempt from the perturbations of space travel with its black holes, warp jumps, and unexpected ripples in the space-time fabric, like the violent rip in the cultural fabric that occurred post-9/11, in which the political universe, while continuing to accelerate technologically, began to curve back to its primal origins in anxiety, distrust, panic, and "bad conscience." This explains why we can live simultaneously in the much-hyped world of global cybernetic development while being embroiled in the most recidivist of fundamentalist religious passions. Today the body of flesh and blood has been literally split in two—part flesh, part machine—with no easy reconciliation on the horizon. Cognitively, we may be the first generation to exist in that peculiar situation bequeathed to those who are truly after Antigone, not only "between living and dying" but already aware that even the language of the prohibited—the excluded—is a constitutive condition for the affirmation of power.

Consequently, when Butler senses the presence everywhere of Nietzsche's contingent power—in gender, sexuality, consciousness, public policy, psychoanalysis—she makes of the *Genealogy* a guide to understanding not only the violent history of the will but also its possible future. For Nietzsche, the debate on the natural and discursive body is a purely "perspectival" event, hiding from view the incorporation of the body by "the passionate attachment to subjection." Call it what you will—the languages of reification, alienation, simulation, and the virtual, or in the more searing terms of Judith Butler, "excretory identities" in an "excretory culture"— today the hint of death is everywhere, animated and seductive but still a resurrection-effect of a culture that only now begins to live. Oscillating wildly between hyperaesthetics and excremental culture, the body desperately clings to any floating sign: the signs of death, panic, fear; the signs of insecurity and instability; but perhaps also the signs of a new multiplicity that is struggling to be born, exist, and thrive.

It is this story of power, this story of *contingent* power, that is recovered by Butler's theoretical imagination. It is, of course, customary to limit understanding power to the logic of inclusions and exclusions. Here the language of exclusions does not operate independently of normative regimes of inclusion but the opposite. Precisely because they are the prohibited—the outcast, the forbidden term—the logic of exclusions designates the essential condition for the affirmation of power. Marking the limits of the psychic life of power, power would no longer operate as a force from the outside—a pressure from the exterior—but as the basic condition of possibility for that which has itself been forbidden. Consequently, *The Psychic Life of Power* can be so politically consequential because it focuses on the doubled nature of power—certainly power from the outside, but more important, the *preontological* constitution of subjectivity by a regime of power that would make of its prohibitions the essential locus of "the passionate attachment to subjection."

Politically, this would culminate in the *paradox* of cynical power—power framed by the apparent oppositions of inclusion and exclusion—that the insurrection of the prohibited (Foucault's famous "insurrection of subjectivity") can never really be confident that the terms of contestation have not been, in fact, staged in advance to amplify the psychic life of power itself. For example, this is the informing logic of Luce Irigaray's evocative theorization of the self-identical logic of masculinist sexuality. It is as well the foundation for Paul Gilroy's insight that the critique of racism is itself constituted, and effectively undermined, by its production as a perspectival effect of the language of racialism itself.

But what if, as in the meditation on power that is the psychic life of Butler, the closed logic of inclusions and exclusions is itself exceeded by a new psychic figuration—a prohibition functioning as its own *singularity-moment*—simultaneously enmeshed in the matrix of power yet all the while expressing something incommensurable? And what if this is not simply creative mimesis but a fatal challenge to power by the emergence of psychic complexity itself? Here the language of the outcast, represented finally only in terms of psychoanalysis, would have something about it of the contingency of life itself, expressing that which cannot be fully absorbed by power yet all the same comprising the most perfect inflection of power. Ironically, what if the lasting importance of *The Psychic Life of Power* is, in the end, not rhetorical but astronomical? Like a massive object in deep, outer space intervening between the human gaze and an otherwise invisible planet to reveal by its very darkness the presence of something otherwise undetectable by human vision, *The Psychic Life of Power* slides between ourselves and that which is otherwise hidden in the astral object of power, lighting up for the first time that which is figurative, fabricated, and creative.

A keen student of contingency, of the vulnerable, the frail, the fragile, Butler's thought begins and ends with the failure of power. Specifically, this is why she can reflect so eloquently about Althusser's concept of interpellation, noting its unique challenge to "being elsewhere or otherwise, without denying our complicity in the law we oppose."[5] Absorbing fully Nietzsche's insight that power always turns back on itself, Butler writes,

> Such possibility would require a different kind of turn, one that, enabled by law, turns away from the law, resisting its lure of identity, an agency that outruns and counters the conditions of its emergence. Such a turn demands a willingness *not* to be—a *critical desubjectivation*—in order to expose the law as less powerful than it seems. . . . How are we to understand the power to be as a constitutive desire? Resituating conscience and interpellation within such an account, we might then add to this question another: However is such a desire exploited not only by law in the singular, but by law of various kinds such that we yield to the temptation in order to maintain some sense of social "being"?
>
> . . . Such a failure of interpellation may well undermine the capacity of the subject to "be" in a self-identical sense, but it may also mark the path toward a more open, even more ethical, kind of being, one of or for the future.[6]

Of this "failure of interpellation," we might question in turn its origins and how the passion for subjection is to be countered by a "critical desubjectivation." Alluding to Jacqueline Rose's utopian gesture toward "unconsciousness as resistance,"[7] to Freud's "post-moral gesture,"[8] which calls into question the values of morality,

Butler has brushed against Nietzsche too deeply not to recognize that the moment of "critical desubjectivation" will have to pass through the psychological storm-center of the bad conscience. For example, speaking of Foucault, she dwells on the paradoxical qualities of the "injurious term":

> He understood that even the most noxious terms could be owned, that the most injurious interpellations could also be the site of radical reoccupation and resignification. But what lets us occupy the site of discursive injury? How are we animated and mobilized by that discursive site and its injury, such that our very attachment to it becomes the condition for our resignification of it?
>
> As a further paradox, then, only by occupying—being occupied by—that injurious term can I resist and oppose it, recasting the power that constitutes me as the power I oppose. In this way, a certain place for psychoanalysis is secured in that any mobilization against subjection will take subjection as its resource, and that attachment to an injurious interpellation will, by way of a necessarily alienated narcissism, become the condition under which resignifying that interpellation becomes possible. This will not be an unconscious outside of power, but rather something like the unconscious of power itself, in its traumatic and productive iterability.[9]

If identity were to be permanently attached to the site of its injury, this would only make of it a site of Nietzsche's bad conscience. But what if there is an "unconscious of power" hidden within the language of power itself as its "traumatic and productive iterability"? And what if the "alienated narcissism" that would emerge from the "failure of interpellation" would take as its challenge not to exceed power from its exterior but to "rework and unsettle the passionate attachment to subjection without which subject formation and re-formation cannot succeed"?[10] For Butler, *being contingent* is the real world of the bad conscience, which is why she can remark of the "chiastic" moment in Nietzsche when the conscience turns back on itself that this is not only "the condition of the possibility of the subject, but the condition of possibility of fiction, fabrication, and transfiguration."[11] Neither a liberal humanist committed to abstract universalism nor a poststructural deconstructionist, Butler occupies a third space in the theorization of power. Silently streaming her thought with other nomadic thinkers before her, she sets out to *undo* interpellation, to *undermine* signification, to *work through* bad conscience, and to do this in a way that is neither universal nor particular but deeply reflexive. Because that is what she truly is—a theorist of psychic complexity—the unconscious of power—seeking to make of the "failure of interpellation" a possible opening to the fictional, the fabricated, the transfigurative. If this makes her a hopeless utopian, it is for all that a utopia of impossibility, which is and, for that matter, has always been the irreducible singularity moment of the human condition.

Of course, in these dark times, utopias, particularly utopias of impossibility, are not permitted. Nietzsche correctly anticipated this when he envisioned a future of suicidal nihilism with its orgies of cynical power led by ascetic priests as "blond beasts of prey," and all this driven onward by the passion for subjection so powerfully captured by the concept of the bad conscience. It is our specific historical fate to actually live today within the body politic thought "posthumously" by Nietzsche, that point where the philosophically universal has been made historically particular. The savagery of the weak will of the "last man" has been realized in political history by what the Pentagon likes to describe as the "long war" of viral terrorism. Metastasizing through the body politic—sometimes assuming the administrative form of hypersurveillance, at other points legitimating itself by apparent threats from the exterior of power—the specter of terrorism has quickly become the "constitutive outside" necessary for the operation of power. Functioning under the sign of cynicism, power flips randomly today from the "homeland" of normative inclusion to an increasingly virulent sense of persecutory anxiety aimed at those nominated for exclusion. Politically unilateral, suspicious of expressions of internal dissent, filled with a crusading sense of missionary consciousness, close-circuiting itself in the domestic bunker, the ambivalent relation of truth and power has now resolved into an epoch of "speaking power to truth." No exceptions are permitted to the logic of the selfsame; no subjectivity is authorized that exceeds normative regimes of inclusion and exclusion; no ethics are allowed that do not privilege the violence of condemnation; no moral perspective is enjoined that does not close ranks with the logic of imperial exceptionalism; and no bodies are to be constituted that are not perfectly mimetic of the ruling standards of representation and intelligibility.

Cautious in her rhetorical claims, pragmatic in her critical aspirations, Butler's utopia of impossibility steers between performativity and lament to discover the third space of a power that would be its own undoing. Her thought draws into presence that which is always most vehemently disavowed by power, namely, the necessary interpellation of figure and ground. Making of her own writing a concept-fiction, an apparent reality, a perspectival simulacrum, she proceeds to undo the disavowal necessary to all power by a strategy of *reflexivity*—Butler's version of Nietzsche's transvaluation of values:

> More precisely, what does it mean to say that a subject emerges only through the action of turning back on itself? If this turning back on oneself is a trope, a movement which is always only *figured* as a bodily movement, but which no body literally performs, in what will the necessity of such a figuration consist? The trope appears to be the shadow of a body, a shadowing of that body's violence against itself, a body in spectral and linguistic form that is the signifying mark of the psyche's emergence.[12]

Noting that there is "no subject except as a consequence of this reflexivity,"[13] Butler begins with a subject trapped in a "logical circularity"—a subject that "appears at once to be presupposed and yet not formed, on the one hand, or formed and hence not presupposed on the other." It is a fully contingent subject born out of a "strange way of speaking"—strange, because like the language of the will turning back on itself before it, "it figures a process which cannot be detached from or understood apart from the figuration."[14] With this fateful conclusion,

> what emerges is not the unshackled will or a "beyond" to power, but another direction for what is most formative in passion, a formative power which is at once the condition of its violence against itself, its status as a necessary fiction, and the site of its enabling possibilities. This recasting of the "will" is not, properly speaking, the will of a subject, nor is it an effect fully cultivated by and through social norms; it is, I would suggest, the site at which the social implicates the psychic in its very formation—or, to be more precise, *as* its very formation and formativity.[15]

Contingent Bodies

> If the term "queer" is to be a site of collective contestation, the point of departure for a set of historical reflections and futural imaginings, it will have to remain that which is, in the present, never fully owned, but always and only redeployed, twisted, queered from a prior usage and in the direction of urgent and expanding political purposes.[16]

So, then, queer bodies are the "site at which the social implicates the psychic in its very formation"—definitely not queer bodies only at the level of the sexual register (although that, too) but queer bodies as a tangible hint of that which is most irrepressible, most present in the moment, most utopian in this doubled language of power as subjection and subjectivation. Here beginning in the psychic economy of gay and lesbian sexuality, mindful of the foreclosures necessary to institute and maintain the hegemony of heterosexual normativity, queer bodies can so easily break the skin barrier because the utopian gesture of "queering" is itself a premonitory sign of the return of the contingent, the ambivalent, the ambiguous. "Never fully owned, and only redeployed twisted, queered from a prior usage," the term *queer* has a more general philosophical, and then political, significance beyond the languages of pleasure and desire. Reversing as a matter of survival the productivist logic of political economy, queer bodies do the impossible by representing a form of power that would be its own undoing. From the foreclosed space of queer sexual economy, from the libidinal energies of gays and lesbians and transsexuals, emerges a counterlogic to the times in which we live, simultaneously its "necessary fiction" and "enabling possibility." Understood retroactively, the future alluded to by the act of queering sex, queering gender, queering politics, has always been with us as that fatal symbolic gesture, the palpable traces of which spread out everywhere today. *Queering history*: that's Walter Benjamin's *Theses on the Philosophy of History,* with its rebellion on behalf of a form of political resistance that would instantly link present and future, making of the forgotten language of the Parisian communard, the Spanish anarcho-syndicalist, the always liquidated poet, the foreclosed space of the artist the avatars of a political history that would stir again, like Klee's *Angel Novalis,* to the storm of the future breaking in on the gathering debris of the past. *Queering ideology*: that's Slavoj Žižek's brilliant, but highly instructive, failure to achieve a radically socialist, radically democratic critique of the elementary *forms* of ideology because he forgot that the sublime object of trauma, this irreducible trace of emptiness, this singular remainder, in the human condition, is always shadowed by the remainder's double—the actual contents, the ambivalent, deeply contested citations—of ideological struggle. *Queering love*: that's Luce Irigaray's *To Be Two,* which introduces a violent, but no less seductive, sudden swerve into the philosophical canons surrounding the question of identity and difference, by recuperating in all its challenge and fragility the ethical demand "to take care of the difference between us, not merely because of its role in generation, because it represents the means of humanity's production and reproduction, but in order to achieve happiness and make it blossom."[17]

In her important essay "Critically Queer," Judith Butler has this to say about drag and the heterosexual imaginary:

> Drag thus allegorizes *heterosexual melancholy,* the melancholy by which a masculine gender is formed from the refusal to grieve the masculine as a possibility of love; a feminine gender is formed (taken on, assumed) through the incorporative fantasy by which the feminine is excluded as a possible object of love, an exclusion never grieved, but "preserved" through the heightening of feminine identification itself. In this sense, the "truest" lesbian melancholic is the strictly straight woman, and the "truest" gay male is the strictly straight male.
>
> What drag exposes is the "normal" constitution of gender presentation in which the gender performed is in many ways constituted by a set of disavowed attachments or identifications that constitute a different domain of the "unperformable." [In a culture of heterosexual melancholy], "The straight man *becomes* (mimes, cites, appropriates, assumes the status of) the man he "never" loved and "never grieved"; the straight woman becomes the woman she "never" loved and "never" grieved. It is in this sense, then, that what is most apparently performed as gender is the sign and symptom of a pervasive disavowal.[18]

It is not just Butler queering gender, adding, that is, to the question of gender a very real element of Lacan's sense of the perverse—making of gender a play of disavowal, melancholy, and foreclosure, on one hand, and undecidability and uncertainty, on the other—but Butler queering as well the question of ideology. Not content with creating real gender trouble by rubbing the panic speech acts of gender as performativity against Luce Irigaray's unspoken, wordless world of sexual desire, this world of "two lips that would be one"; definitely not ready to settle for a compromised world of bodies that matter, with what is an exclusively *theoretical* explanation that posits embodiment as the polar opposite of gender (lesbian and gay sexuality as that which is necessarily foreclosed, never grieved, never loved by the straight man and the straight woman, the straight world, that is, of compulsive heterosexual normativity as drag on speed); and not content to reinscribe the boundaries between gender, bodies, and sex that all her writing has struggled to deconstruct, Judith Butler is that rarity of a thinker, a theorist of whom it might be said what Heidegger once remarked about Nietzsche, that in his thought first he would argue, and Butler's next I would argue, there is to be found a theoretical imaginary that represents the self-overcoming of the respective cultures in which they lived. In Heidegger's perspective, Nietzsche's thought, represented in all its passion and denials in *The Gay Science, The Twilight of the Idols, On the Genealogy of Morals, Thus Spake Zarathustra,* and *The Will to Power,* represents the self-overcoming of nihilism; Judith Butler's self-overcoming is more complex. Certainly her theorisations represent the self-overcoming of heterosexual normativity in favor of a form of thought that is radically, playfully, passionately—critically—queer, but something else, too, something else in her thought that is just at the other edge of queer politics; something that is not exclusively about the compulsive, mimed, cited, appropriated mechanisms of compulsive heterosexuality; something that goes beyond even the still unexplored sexualities of gays, lesbians, and trannies; something that in Nietzsche's words is human, all-too-human; a haunting aporia that has to do with a fatal pause in Butler's theoretical project. Who knows why? Maybe it's the inexplicability in straight–queer discourse of comprehending the full dimensions of the gathering darkness of the human condition—sites of bodily and cultural injury used now as political opportunities for projecting all the madness of ressentiment onto an always crusading, always missionary, never grieving, never loving, reanimated world historical project of American imperialism. Or perhaps Butler's thought was fatally undermined by all those disappeared bodies that really did matter to her—the bodies of the ethnically scapegoated, those bodies trapped in "indefinite detention," the bodies of the disappeared, the oppressed, bodies that are ethically rendered in the grisly terms of Heidegger as objects of "*abuse value,*" bodies that exemplify the exact opposite of Levinas' resurrection of the face as the basis of an ethics of responsibility, namely, bodies reduced to the cruel ethical tutelary of the "*injurious neglect of the thing.*"[19]

Now given the certain uncertainty of the human heart and the undecidability of any individual human's response to a time of real political emergency, I don't know, or perhaps have no real need to know, the genealogy of Butler's self-overcoming, that point where her thought came to represent the self-overcoming of being critically queer in the direction of something that touches deeply not simply our sexual condition but our human condition—*being critically human.*

I do know this. Under the impress of the gathering darkness, her thought has changed, has mutated from the mirror of gender and the rhetoric of excitable speech to something more intangible, more uncertain, and more ethically responsive. Perhaps this transformation was prefigured in the title of one of her books—*Precarious Life: The Powers of Mourning and Violence.* Or perhaps Butler moving from *queering gender* with memories of bodies that matter to Butler *queering ideology* with memories of *Precarious Life* is prefigured by something else, by a political register in her thought which, until now, was always foreclosed, excluded, never really noticed. Perhaps the entire theoretical project of Judith Butler specifically and of the queer community generally has always been in the way of a complex prefiguring, a premonitory rehearsal in the codes of panic gender and prohibited sexualities, of a more ominous turn in contemporary ideology—not just drag now in its exclusive gender citations as an index of that which is foreclosed by the straight man and the straight woman of all the club scenes but an entire political culture that is in *imperial drag,* that generalizes the psychoanalytics of compulsive heterosexuality from the theater of sexual representation to the theater of world politics. All the signs of compulsive heterosexuality are there—panic responses to the contamination of bodily fluids that was the immediate response to HIV have now become surveillance strategies of the new biometric state; the hysterical male who thrives in faith-based politics with its panic about same-sex marriage and fear of, and seduction by, gay desire; and all the unmourned, ungrieved violence that is the everyday life experience of women suffering domestic violence and of disappeared sex workers and gays and lesbians and trannies when they walk the streets of *Stone Butch Blues.* What is all this but a vast, inflected rehearsal in the language of sexual denial and compulsory gender performativity of a political culture that functions now by displacing its previously isolated sexual politics onto its imperial missionary ambitions—and in a straight way, too. Power now is always in drag, always performing that which it refuses to love, to grieve, to mourn. Power now is heterosexual melancholy in its most dangerous phase: that ambivalent stage of triumphant self-recognition of its own fierce strength and panicked self-denial about those bodies, those sexualities, those "faces" of Levinas, those memories it must de-cite, disappropriate, de-index if it is to flourish.

Now, in the first stage of this story of nihilism, Nietzsche came on stage to play the part of the madman in the marketplace who announces the death of God. In the final stage of nihilism, completed nihilism, the projection of heterosexual melancholy as the spearhead of contemporary political history, it's not Nietzsche of *The Gay Science* and *The Twilight of the Idols* who appears on stage but Nietzsche in drag, Nietzsche channeled through Judith Butler to perform the "unperformable," Nietzsche's prophecy of nihilism mimed and cited and appropriated by Judith Butler as a way, perhaps the only way, of bringing into presence that which is excluded and foreclosed by an imperial politics of compulsive heterosexual performativity.

And why not? Butler's rhetoric always plays the game of the doubled sign. Not Lordship and Bondage but something more complicated, something that makes of gender, sex, ideology, and power the incommensurable politics of the performative. In her writing, not only gender but the whole compulsive language of phantasmatic identification is burning. Butler can write so eloquently about the lesbian phallus because in her thought the meaning of being queer has escaped its exclusively sexual register to become the burning sign of the unconscious of a power that is never about the real as lack but rather real bodies, real injuries, real sexualities as sites of foreclosure and contestation.

Contingent Violence: Indefinite Detention, Suicide Bombers, and Surveillance Cameras

Most unusual, and certainly noteworthy, about the thought of Judith Butler is that her intellectual project is fully suspended between critical proximity to the larger issues of contemporary political ethics and a gathering intimation, present in all her reflections, that we are witness today to a larger cultural crisis, one that may find brutal expression in the disappeared subjects and abused bodies of the imperial reign of power but that has its basis in the origin story of the Christian self. In her writing, it is as if the fabric of space-time itself splits open, bringing into presence the more profound dimensions of a cultural crisis that, while expressed most brutally in "excitable speech" as political ethics, is deeply inflected with the more infelicitous language of metaphysics.

Everywhere Butler's thought touches on the urgent questions of contemporary political ethics: issues related to indefinite detention, media censorship, suicide bombers, Islamic religious martyrs, ubiquitous surveillance cameras in an infinitely receding war on terror, the resurgence of Christian fundamentalism in the politically potent form of crusading, missionary consciousness, and the bitterness of the heart that may well represent an early sign of a coming global reaction on the part of the dispossessed against the excesses of capitalism under the sovereign sign of imperialism.

Reflecting on the political context that gave rise to the political ethics of *Precarious Life: The Powers of Mourning and Violence,* we can acknowledge with confidence that some historical tendencies are now effectively completed. For example, the twentieth-century experiment in the politics of late modernity—the illusion of a bipolar world frozen in the hegemonic codes of communism versus capitalism, American versus Soviet empires—ended decisively with the fall of the Berlin Wall in 1989. Indeed, the city of Berlin can rise once again as a major cultural capital of the West because on that night in 1989, the political history of the twenty-first century effectively began. Ours would be a future not bipolar but multipolar, not capitalism versus communism but one driven by the specter of capitalism triumphant, which, finally liberated of its constraining binary of socialism, would finally be open to seduction by the siren call of its always repressed, always present dark underside—fascism. Already wing strokes can be heard in the nighttime air of Hegel's owl of Minerva returning to the political history from which it first took flight.

And something else has been completed as well. In the short interval between the fall of the Berlin Wall and the violent events of 9/11 in New York and Washington, D.C., another world historical project—the much hyped new world order of globalization—quickly rose and just as suddenly disappeared. Perhaps it was the global protests of student activists, workers, feminists, and environmentalists who revolted in the late 1990s against the policing regime of the World Trade Organization and the International Monetary Fund; or maybe it was the revolt from the south—the electoral rebellion of popular forces in Bolivia, Peru, and Venezuela—that rose against the manifest destiny of U.S. hegemony; or perhaps it was the countergift of a bodily death that cannot be refused by Islamic religious martyrs—what Bataille once described as the gift of the "accursed share"—that finally broke the solipsistic power of empire. As the Chicago political theorist Michael A. Weinstein has argued, globalization was always just the bait dangled to hook the world on a diet of consumer capitalism. When that did not work, the politics of American political unilateralism was immediately called on to jam the hook of compulsory capitalism down the throat of an often unwilling global population. For all the discussion today concerning the digital wonders of information technology and the information economy, what increasingly now prevails is the logic of primitive capitalism and predatory power.

Consequently, political paradoxes proliferate. For example, at the same instant futurist genetic laboratories are conjuring android successors to the human species, the remainder of the all-too-human species lives in a growing archipelago of radical destitution and despair—Mike Davis' *Planet of Slums* with its one billion occupants denied the most minimal forms of recognition and reciprocity. Or consider the rhetoric of *panic terror* that dominates the administrative apparatus of homeland security in most of the countries of the Western world. Panic terror? That's the contemporary counterreaction of hegemonic binaries with a strict normative logic of inclusion and exclusion. In an age of intense securitization, the system of power itself is increasingly haunted by paranoiac fears of revenge by those who have been excluded from the spectacle of consumption. A hauntology of the dispossessed, the excluded, and those violently excommunicated from the Western ethical order of the "human" remains the most pervasive psychological feature of imperial power. This could also explain why there now takes place the active criminal prosecution in the United States of over two hundred postmodern artists. Their apparent crime? In a time of heightened security, control of the symbolic framework is everything. Understood in these terms, postmodern artists are always necessarily sign-criminals. By its very aesthetic nature, postmodern art works to disturb dominant frameworks of un-derstanding—transgressing boundaries, privileging the complex, the hybrid, the incommensurable. When the specter of an art of complexity haunts power, then we finally know that we are living in the final days of a fully nihilistic power.

In these dark times, a sense of apocalypse surrounding the tri-umph of Nietzsche's "last man" is everywhere. After five hundred years of technological abuse—making of nature what Nietzsche said would be a future of cruel experiments and vivisectioning—nature itself has finally rebelled. In the twenty-first century, this great rebellion of nature will likely be played out in the increas-ingly catastrophic scenarios of global climate change. For all the predictions concerning the fast disappearance of the body at the behest of cybernetic technology, images of the very material body are everywhere—hostage bodies, bodies that are genocided, tagged, biochipped, surveilled, and electronically scanned. But for all that, bodies always incarnate a wayward heart, an irrepressible spark of individuality that is capable always and anywhere of suddenly rising to seek a greater truth. Precarious life can only arise again in union with an equally precarious nature.

It is precisely the global political crisis that makes the lessons of Butler's *Precarious Life* so astute, producing a lucid meditation on the psychic reality that is simultaneously the precondition and object of contemporary politics. An American confessional, this book does that which is as improbable as it is difficult. In a solitary, courageous act of speaking truth to power, *Precarious Life* inter-rogates, first and foremost, the origins of the malice of strife in the wounded American heart. Here the psychological formations present in contemporary displays of a near-universal state of injury, unfathomable rage, a "narcissistic preoccupation with melancholia," hostility toward the Other, the alien, the immigrant, is dissected with a logic that is as psychoanalytically clinical as it is emotion-ally remorseless. Nothing is spared—not the executive branch of government, which is held to exploit public grieving for its own predetermined political ends; not the judiciary, who are found as being receptive to politically prescribed limits on free speech at the behest of the new security state; not the larger majority of the voting public, which has made its private compromises with the carceral politics of indefinite detention, surveillance cameras, and the suppression of inconvenient truths; and certainly not the mass media, which is exposed not for excessive indulgence in the lesser games of image manipulation but for the more problematic ethical issue of "evacuating the human through the image." Always a faithful political student of the incommensurability of power, it is Butler's thesis that the will to violence today is supported, not so much by the effacement of the Other, but by a media strategy of continuously calling up the face of the Other—the Afghan woman, the political dissident, the always fugitive immigrant—only to instantly dehumanize her. Like power itself, the visual norm of the human contains the usual double logic of simultaneous representation and disappearance, *nomination* as the specter of the unrepresentable and *designation* as the visual symbol of primitive victimization, terror, porous borders, incomprehensible resistance:

> Indeed, all of these images seem to suspend the precariousness of life; they either represent American triumph, or provide an incitement for American military triumph in the future. *They are the spoils of war or they are the targets of war.* And in this sense, we might say that the face is, in every instance, defaced, and that this is one of the representational and philosophical consequences of war itself.[20]

Butler can undertake such a searing confessional of American psychic reality, faithfully transcribing the deepest interiority of the American mind—its psychic oscillations between fear and the technological sublime—because her thought has always been inflected with what Foucault once described as a "language of descent," a form of thought that, while brushing against the immediacy of political life, follows a deeper trajectory to the metaphysical origins of the crisis of precarious life. Consequently, if in books such as *Excitable Speech* and *Precarious Life*, Butler diagnoses so accurately the self-confirming logic of inclusion and exclusion that circuits power today, it is because her project has never been posterior to the question of political ethics but philosophically anticipatory of the contemporary crisis of nihilism. It is no coincidence that she so brilliantly recovers the haunting voice of Antigone, not only as a way of critiquing political authority but as a means of rupturing the language of power supportive of the psychic reality of oedipalization. For example, Butler concludes *Precarious Life* with a prophecy and a warning phrased in the classical language of lament:

> If the humanities has a future as cultural criticism, and cultural criticism has a task at the present moment, it is no doubt to return us to the human where we do not expect to find it, in its frailty and at the limits of its capacity to make sense. We would have to interrogate the emergence and vanishing of the human at the limits of what we can know, what we can hear, what we can see, what we can sense. This might prompt us, affectively, to reinvigorate the intellectual projects of critique, of questioning, of coming to understand the difficulties and demands of cultural translation and dissent, and to create a sense of the public in which oppositional voices are not feared, degraded, or dismissed, but valued for the instigation to a sensate democracy they occasionally perform.[21]

In these words can be heard once again the dissenting voice of Antigone, speaking kinship to authority, responsibility to cynicism, affirming against the hard winds of political power the possibility of those indispensable virtues of the human, those *human* frailties that have long been practiced as the limit experiences of reciprocity, love, and compassion. While these frailties may function "at the limits of [their] capacity to make sense," perhaps this is because the human begins, now as always, with that which is beyond sense, with those fragments of life that have somehow succeeded in revolting against the spirit-flesh of power that circuits our bodies, cultures, and politics.

Antigone's Nietzsche

This reflection on contingency in the philosophy of Judith Butler would be incomplete if it didn't seek to make of its own interpretative strategies a fully contingent inquiry, concluding with a question to which, while there may be no satisfactory response, there remains an indubitable, and entirely satisfying, element of doubt: is it possible that all of Butler's work to date has been in the order of a great preparation for another philosophical task, one not consciously adopted nor theoretically designated but one to which the question to which all of Butler's thought is a continuing response—namely, how to make *unfinished* the closed rhetoric of sex, bodies, power, gender, and knowledge—inevitably recurs, and on behalf of which Butler's thought is of necessity simultaneously classically ancient and posthuman in equivalent degrees? Is it possible that Butler's thought has effectively never been after Nietzsche, *but always before Nietzsche?* Does Butler's continuing meditation on the crisis of split subjectivity represent in all its intensity the main problematic to which all of Nietzsche's thought struggled to respond? Indeed, if Butler can write so passionately about the complex translations and dissents of being human today, about the frailty of the human condition, does the reason for this have less to do with the urgency of her political analysis than the fact that her thought is the privileged site at which a deeper crisis in the modern project has broken out once again?

Definitely not nostalgic, Butler can enjoin the question of the human as an effective riposte to a form of power that would make the human disappear because her writing effectively seeks to complete in advance Nietzsche's *On the Genealogy of Morals.* And how could it not? Butler's impassioned recurrence to the voice of Antigone, her brushing *Bodies That Matter* against *Gender Trouble,* her exploration of *The Psychic Life of Power,* and her ethics written out in the pages of *Precarious Life* and *Excitable Speech* represent the horizon of a critical philosophy of completed nihilism written at the height of its times. Here we find ourselves engaged in a language of descent that draws thought downward to the gravity well of *On the Genealogy of Morals.* But not concluding with Nietzsche, or should we say not impeded by the received interpretation of Nietzsche as an early student of normalized power, Butler's is a form of thought that actually follows the fatal glance of Nietzsche as he follows his own language of descent to the Christian origins of the genealogy of morals. Indeed, given the uncertain direction of time's arrow in the passage of thought from one writer to another in the great chain of philosophical being, Butler may not so much follow Nietzsche as actually precede Nietzsche by illuminating the genealogy of the crisis of split subjectivity.

In Butler's Nietzsche, it is the figure of Antigone who haunts *Genealogy,* and it is precisely by uncovering the Antigone in Nietzsche that Butler traces Nietzsche's own descent into the psychic reality of the human-all-too-human. Here the genealogy of the human is finally brought into presence: not only the distinctive human instinct for revenge taking—*being reversed against itself in self-loathing*—that forms the basis of so much of contemporary politics but something more ominous, namely, constituting the modern subject on the anvil of the death of instinctual behavior and the politics of reactive being. In Butler's thought, there is a very real *political problematic,* specifically, that the same metaphysical crisis to which all of Nietzsche's thought represented a sustained response has broken out again in the form of contemporary American empire politics; and there is an equally real *political ethic*—the reworking of the politics of reactive being and the death of instinctual behavior with the rhetoric of that which is for all its frailties indispensably human: *Antigone's Nietzsche.*

Nietzsche may have written *On the Genealogy of Morals* in 1887, but the cultural context out of which the book appears itself has a longer descent, a genealogical trace bringing together texts from the fourth and the twentieth centuries, namely, Augustine's *Confessions* as the book that *Genealogy* interpellates. More than anything, *Genealogy* immediately revolts against the traditional canons of philosophy, beyond critiques of Plato and Kant, to directly engage the conditions under which morality itself is staged, namely, the conditions under which Christian confessionality first created the modern subject as we know it, and once having been set in place, this subject has at once become both condition and end of all valuing.

With the *Genealogy,* we descend deeply into the repressed dreams of modernity, where that which is most ancient (debates between Athanasius and Ambrose, Augustine's predecessors in fourth-century North Africa as Bishops of Carthage, battling the heresy of Arianism, with its implicit denial that Christ is the Son of God and thus the living Incarnation of the Holy Spirit) and this which is most futuristic (our abiding faith in scientific rationality played out now most hysterically in the search by contemporary physicists for "God's Particle" as the most elementary force of nature) are brought together in a genealogy of morals, past, present, and future. There are always three bodies circulating in the *Genealogy*— *spirit-flesh* ("the soul stretched as a membrane across the confessional self"), *mnemotechnic flesh* (how subjects are rendered "regular, calculable" by the power of the modern state through the propadeutic practice of burning remembrance into conscience by making it hurt to forget), and bodies constituted by the *will to truth* (inscribing consciousness with the mythic aims of a science that would deny its own foundations in mythology). Nietzsche is a genealogist whose thought descends into the gray matter of these three sedimented strata of the modern subject.

How could it be otherwise? More than a strictly religious impulse that would eventually war with the language of scientific rationality, Christian confessionality represented a successful metaphysical resolution to a paralyzing cultural crisis that neither philosophy nor secular culture could resolve. This crisis—the crisis of radically divided experience with power, represented by Roman pragmatism on the one side and reason figured by Athenian tragedy on the other—evaded all pragmatic resolutions that were only *externally* posited. Power itself could never provide a satisfactory response to the compelling existential question, namely, now that we have won an empire, now that we have conquered the world with spear and axe, what are to be the ultimate ends of the will to power itself? And reason also, which even in the noblest moments of Epicurean sensibility could never discover an adequate rejoinder to the question concerning the ultimate ends of reason: why is it that a life of reason is not to culminate in a universe of the absurd?

It was precisely at the moment of greatest crisis—power without substantive purpose and reason tinged by the absurd—that the Christian formulation first appeared, provoking in its wake the great debate among Rome, Athens, and Jerusalem. Represented in all its religious passion, yet philosophical subtlety, by the Trinitarian formula—God the Father, God the Son, and God the Holy Ghost, in other words, by the signifying logic of will, intelligence, and affect—Christianity moved the metaphysical center of Western experience from power and reason on the outside, externally posited, to the most intimate moment of interiority, the *directly experienced* confessionality of the Christian subject. Henceforth the internal principle of unity of Western experience would not be the instrumentalism of power without ultimate ends or reason without limits but that momentous fusion of conversionary belief, apostolic action, and determined will power that became first the Christian subject and later, when the entire horizon had been wiped clean of the language of the sacred, the modern subject. With the invention of the Christian self, *personality* was made the creative principle of will, intelligence, and affect—simultaneously a redemptive sign of salvation and a psychic foreclosure against sinfulness. Here being human would come to mean *being spirit-flesh,* being possessed fully by the power of Incarnation. Henceforth the will to power would be animated by the *death of wild, instinctual behavior* and the *triumph of reactive being.* In the form of the will to power, the reduction of being human to spirit-flesh would be repeated daily as the overriding psychic reality of modernity.

Just as Nietzsche's *Zarathustra* was a parodic rewriting of the New Testament, the *Genealogy,* with its three enigmatic essays— "'Good and Evil,' 'Good and Bad'"; "'Guilt,' 'Bad Conscience' and the Like"; and "What Is the Meaning of Ascetic Ideals?"—is itself a parody of the Christian Trinity, with "god the father as the source of all evil" as the subject of the first essay; God the Son, this fateful sign of sacrificial violence and the origin of all ressentiment, as the subject matter of the second essay; and the Holy Ghost, the ascetic ideal, as the meaning of the third essay. Stated in a more liturgical way, to read the *Genealogy* is to participate in Nietzsche's parodic reenactment of the great Christian rituals of Good Friday, Holy Saturday, and Easter Sunday, with this patient, gray genealogy of the complex subject who appears under the sign of the "cross, the nut, and the light," this subject who is constituted by ressentiment, by what Heidegger will later call a "malice of strife," who first carried out a relentless vivisectioning of his every motive ("cruelty turned inwards," "itching for revenge," "feeling bad about himself," always eager for "orgies of feeling" associated with the great spectacles of sacrificial violence), and who only awaits for its ressentiment to be given a direction by Nietzsche's "ascetic priests," the keepers of ascetic ideals).

With the appearance of the self-identical subject formed out of the crucible of Christian confessionality, we find ourselves suddenly in the presence of a deeply paradoxical self. Undoubtedly influenced by Foucault's interpretation of Nietzsche, but definitely exceeding Foucault's understanding of the radical implications of *Genealogy,* Butler demonstrates in all her writing that the real issues today are not limited to issues of body and discipline nor to the migration of power as death to power as life. Anterior to these concerns, although obscured by the religious discourse of confessionality, there remains that enigmatic quality that Nietzsche identified in the *Genealogy* under the sign of the "transvaluation of values," which is to say that the subject, whether the subject of the fourth-century Christian confessional or the modern subject of *Precarious Life,* only emerges, indeed *can* only emerge, through the action of *turning back on itself.* For the modern subject no less than the Christian confessional self, the triumph of purely reactive being and the death of instinctual behavior is its psychic essence.

I want to suggest that everything in Butler's thought has been in the order of an intense preparation for understanding the full dimensions of the cultural crisis of the split subject. Consequently, if I have dwelt on the genealogy of the *Genealogy,* it is with the dual purpose of privileging the missing mass of Christianity as Nietzsche's hauntology and also to note that after Nietzsche, Butler is the one contemporary theorist fully alert to the psychic genealogy of the Christian self and its radical implications for the constitution of the modern subject. When she speaks about the appearance of a self that turns back on itself, about the creation of a fully fictitious self as the constitutive vocabulary of modernism, about the immersion of the psyche in the social, her thought is fully present with Nietzsche's at the moment of the Augustinian resolution of the crisis of split subjectivity. After all, the original formulation of the "logical circularity" of the modern subject is to be discovered in the confessional self whereby the goal of the confessional self is also its abiding justification.

Butler studies in the twenty-first century key precisely what happens when the circularity of the self-identical subject breaks down—the violence of *Precarious Life,* the struggles of *Bodies That Matter,* the dissents of *Gender Trouble,* the voices of *Excitable Speech,* and the human reciprocity of *Antigone's Claim.* True to her own claims on behalf of that which is undecidable, uncertain, doubtful, hesitating in the bodily conditions of an always frail human community, Butler's lasting achievement is to make of the quality of *being unfinished* a double moment of danger and enablement. When the modern subject turns back on itself only to find, in its past as much as in its future, a psyche that has been inhabited by spirit-flesh, a body invested by the pain of mnemotechnics, and a will to truth edging toward cynicism and abuse value, then Butler's injunctions on behalf of *Precarious Life* are also appeals on behalf of the small, fragile mercies of precarious thought.

3

COMPLEXITIES:
THE POSTHUMAN SUBJECT
OF KATHERINE HAYLES

With the writings of Katherine Hayles, complexity theory is transformed from its origins in the scientific epistēmē, becoming the basis of a worldview that not only grounds the study of electronic textuality in a "new materialism" but also transforms the concept of complexity itself into the essence of a more comprehensive vision of culture, society, and the body.

Refusing to honor traditional divisions between science and literature, Hayles' thought does that which is more difficult, yet ultimately more insightful. Her theoretical analysis actually folds the very latest configurations in the new science of complexity together with literature (both print and electronic) to the delirious point where "information loses its body." But for all that, the new body that emerges—the *posthuman body*—discovers in the accelerated rhythms of scientific discovery an improved vocabulary for understanding what is happening to its subjectivity, perception, and memory as it is fast-processed through the digital matrix. By all accounts, Hayles should be yet just another theorist following the pilgrim's journey of the virtual body, but there is something recalcitrant, deeply scientific, even bodily in her perspective that refuses easy closure. Indeed, her thought always performs at the edge of incommensurability, theorizing the logic of virtuality as a sign of a newly emergent materialism. With this, a new universe of living and nonliving matter surfaces in her writings—a fluid world of inscriptions, supplementarity, fast traces, folded histories, and paradoxical perspectives. Methodologically, she can do this because she has made of her own thought a field of instability. What she has theorized in *The Cosmic Web*—namely, understanding the *force fields* of science as key to interpreting the new literature of Nabokov and Pynchon—what she has meticulously researched in *How We Became Posthuman,* what she has visualized in *My Mother Was a Computer* and *Writing Machines,* she has first done to her own theoretical perception. A force field accelerating across the space-time spectrum of digital reality, the theoretical imagination of Katherine Hayles, with its alliances with science fiction, linguistic theory, and chaotics, is perhaps the closest approximation we have yet experienced concerning how digital reality chooses to disclose itself today.

Chaos, Catastrophe, Complexity, Crash

For over sixty years, complexity theory has generated a persistent line of scientific questioning that, focusing intently on the question of change, has sought to analyze those elusive moments in which the real world of computation—the world of bifurcations, dissipative structures, broken boundaries, fractals, and fluidities—undergoes a dramatic morphological change of state. In its earlier formulation by the Swiss theorist René Thom, attention to instantly morphological changes of state was eloquently captured by the emblematic vision of chaos theory. Here, rejecting the binary divisions of normal science having to do with science and code, analysis focused on those almost undetectable, but momentous, pattern changes in the nature of things whereby supposedly solid matter suddenly dissolved into dynamic process and beautifully chaotic fractures opened up in the deep structures of everyday life. While this prescient European formulation of complexity theory was ultimately doomed to have its creative vision concerning the dynamic complexity of living and nonliving beings flatlined by later, more romanticized visions of chaotics, its focus on the fluidity of all matter, the mutability of all patterns, and the order within chaos succeeded in being passed on in later iterations of cybernetic theory. In a general sense, the terms are interchangeable—chaos, catastrophe, complexity, crash— but the basic sensibility that informs this intellectual insurgency remains the same, namely, that so-called structures of regularity and patterns of order are only aesthetic mise-en-scènes distracting attention from the self-organizing, self-energizing deep currents of chaotics as the legacy norms of all living and nonliving matter.

Like an intellectual virus, some variation of complexity theory has always represented the hauntology of modern, postmodern, and now posthuman theory.

In an almost biblical sense, chaos theory begets catastrophe theory; catastrophe theory begets complexity theory; and crash is always the word made flesh. Whether chaotic changes of state, "punctuated catastrophes," or the "intermediations" of complexity theory, the reality of computation has required a theory of morpho- logical changes of state capable of explaining the newly emergent realities of digital culture, including the meaning of human sub- jectivity as it is caught up in a web of "relational processing" and "ubiquitous computing." When code circulates in the slipstream of data moving at light speed, it undergoes strange perturbations: moving sideways, losing its (physical) referents only to gain a new (electronic) body, inscribing itself in the materiality of human flesh, here interpellating the eye of perception, there zooming outward to become the generalized surveillance operator of codes and power. Harbingers of creative chaos, punctuated catastrophe, and complexity, the real world of code is what happens when light speed and light power become the skin of society.

But for all this, the story of code does not escape, and can never escape, the labyrinth of history. Obsessed with creating endur- ing patterns of social order and regimes of political security in response to the violent centrifugal pressures of medieval religious conflict, chaos is the hauntology of the modern era. This is why the binary stars of chaos and order can so nicely frame the mod- ernist debate, where the sign of chaos is privileged as an almost fetishistic substitute for the insolvable problems of internecine religious conflict. Equally, catastrophe theory is the capstone of postmodernism. If postmodernism is visualized as a general multidisciplinary critique—spanning architecture, cinema, video, and music to literature, politics, and social ecology—focused on the death of referentiality, then images of catastrophe in film, science, and literature perfectly capture the specter of hauntology that is postmodernism itself, while simultaneously energizing a system viewed as dying of its own lack of meaning. As contemporary history migrates from the catastrophic specter of postmodernism to the transformative sensibility of posthumanism, the sign of catastrophe folds quickly into complexity. Where catastrophe signified the death of the referentials, complexity is different. It indicates that the borderlines between death and life, identity and difference, are inherently unstable, porous, permeable, and that what lies in the balance is the energetic renewal of the dense materiality of being itself. Literally, complexity is a fractal of catastrophe, a deviation from the eternal story of chaos, holding out the promise of an ecological adjustment in the laminar flows of energy itself. And crash? That's the specter of hauntology that always accompanies the violent convergences of modernism, postmodernism, and posthumanism. Here the twisted strands of chaos, catastrophe, and complexity evade all attempts at historical periodization, finding expression as minute, but explosive, fracture points whereby modernist hopes meet postmodern skepticism and the postmodern critique of cynical reason undermines and is, in turn, undermined by the fabulist tale of complexity.

With reference to the specific topic of this essay—the posthuman subject of Katherine Hayles—the convergence and struggle among chaos, catastrophe, complexity, and crash are important premonitory signs. If Hayles' thought creates, as I believe it does, the posthuman subject out of the tangled web of chaotics and complexity, this intimates in advance that some measure will also have to be taken of those missing lacunae of the posthuman subject—the doubled vectors of (postmodern) catastrophe and (hypermodern) crash. But then again, raising critical questions concerning the death of the referentials and the terrorism of the code is not peculiar to Hayles' intellectual trajectory. Indeed, concern with the sheer complexity of information both in terms of its possibilities and degradations has a lengthy pedigree in American letters. For example, we have only to consider the quintessentially American tradition of pragmatism, including most notably the writings of William James *(Essays in Radical Empiricism)* and John Dewey *(Reconstruction in Philosophy),* which set the stage, epistemologically speaking, for the privileging of dynamic process, not stability, in social theory. Refusing both the dogmatic closures of religious belief and the reductions of behavioral sensationalism, James' focus on the "buzzing, blooming field of human experience," with its complex relations, deep processes, and fluid perturbations, inspired later generations of American researchers to focus on the dynamic imminence of human action. While this streak of pragmatic naturalism in American intellectuality would eventually find its capstone in a style of social theory that attempted in effect to smash the atoms of human action (Talcott Parsons' *The Structure of Social Action*), it was left to the theoretical imagination of Katherine Hayles to succeed where so many had failed before. In a contemporary political context that bears remarkable similarities to that of the early days of American pragmatism, with its crowded social field of religious fundamentalists and resurgent positivists, Hayles raises once again the challenge of any vision of the humanities that would be paradigmatic, namely, how to construct the creative posthuman subject out of the Charybdis of (modern) chaos and (posthuman) complexity, while avoiding the Scylla of (postmodern) catastrophe and (hypermodern) crash.

The Return of Lucretius

Indeed, if the theoretical imagination of Katherine Hayles can have such an animating quality, attracting critical attention both by its intellectual eloquence and theoretical creativity, it may also be due to the fact that there is something *metaphysical* at stake in her overall project. While her thought explores the future of leading-edge posthuman culture, an intangible trace of something philosophically ancient is present in the performative conditions of her inquiry. She is arguably the latest exponent of a line of scientific thought originating in the first century A.D., wherein the political turbulence of a Roman Empire in decline was matched by the brilliant epicurean naturalism of Lucretius' *On the Nature of the Universe.* Here Lucretius, refusing both the static equilibrium of Greek scientific naturalism and the superstitious appeal to the gods of the Roman imperium, created a theory of the natural universe predicated on unpredictability, irregularity, and creative catastrophes. For Lucretius, then, as for Hayles now, it is in the nature of (electronic) nature to take sudden "swerves" rather than stabilizing fatalistically in permanent patterns of entropy. Whether a Roman epicurean naturalist like Lucretius or an American complexity theorist like Hayles, both are confronted by the problem of stasis—Lucretius by a theory of "atomism" that permitted no moment of imminent change, Hayles by the fatal specter of the second law of thermodynamics.

In her insightful account of the cultural history of nonlinear dynamics, the British cultural theorist Susan Mapstone has called attention to Lucretius' poetic utterance in favor of the "clinamen or the swerve"—"this minute deviation"—in the nature of things:[1]

> If it were not for this swerve, everything would fall downwards like raindrops through the abyss of space. No collision would take place and no impact of atom upon atom would be created. Thus nature would never have created anything.[2]

Always a migrant tendency hovering on the margins of normal science, Lucretian naturalism has finally come into its own in the twenty-first century in the technological form of electronic textuality. It's as if cyberculture, what Hayles describes as the "regime of computation," is made for the Lucretian "swerve." Here the transformation of the space-time fabric moving at the speed of light into the deep technical materiality of culture, society, and economy privileges not only the smooth flows of the data stream but also those multiple fluctuations where "minute deviations" in data transmission amplify into social change of a far greater magnitude. For example, from the perspective of power, RSS chips, intended to facilitate consumer marketing, instantly become a potentially powerful tool of government surveillance. Deep mining the data archive mutates into a primary weapon in the early detection of possible security threats and, in the process, sweeps away traditional civil liberties as technologically, which is to say *politically,* irrelevant. In terms of economics, "minute deviations" in software programming, such as file-to-file sharing, immediately unleash a profound revolution in economic affairs, instantly undermining traditional structures of intellectual property rights in music, cinema, and publishing. In the contemporary regime of computation, what counts is the fluctuation, the software bifurcation, the digital swerve, the mutation in the stream, the static in the code.

Consequently, if it seems strange to begin a critical appraisal of the contribution of the thought of Katherine Hayles—a preeminent theorist living at the intellectual tip of the technological spearhead of American empire—to understanding embodied culture today, that is perhaps because we have not yet fully absorbed Heidegger's insight that that which seems to be furthest from our particular history is often, in fact, closest at hand. Like Lucretius, Hayles' theoretical challenge rests on a single-minded concentration on the minute deviation, the swerve, the fluctuation, the perturbation in the nature of things. Also like Lucretius, Hayles, writing in turbulent political times, refuses to rest her (theoretical) case on either the entropic tendencies of Newtonian mechanics or on nostalgic mythologies concerning the approaching era of "technological singularities." Neither a scientific mechanist nor a philosophical monist, Hayles' mind is that most rare of incommensurabilities—a fluctuation in the intellectual space-time fabric of the data stream that has managed to transform a theoretical appreciation of "minute deviations" in the nature of the (American) universe into an intellectually compelling history of electronic textuality *(Writing Machines)*, a brilliant rethinking of liberal subjectivity in relationship to the era of computation *(How We Became Posthuman)*, and an evocative account of the data stream that has now become our shared literary homeland *(My Mother Was a Computer)*. With its concentration on the critical transformation of scientific creativity into a new style of electronic literary criticism combined with a certain skepticism toward the knowability of "unexecutable code," Hayles' thought transforms Lucretius' "swerve" into the operating system of the global (digital) brain.

Out of Chaos, "Non-Order"

Exactly like the chaotics of which she is a superb analyst, Hayles' thought represents a creative fluctuation in the order of things. At stake is not only a critical reconsideration of the relationship of literature and science but something of greater cultural significance. It's as if in the intellectual persona of a humanities professor interested in the impact of the "regime of computation" on culture, society, and politics, her thought reveals a broader ontological vista: dissipative structures, bifurcation, recursive symmetry, strange attractors, nonlinear dynamics, life that exists "far from equilibrium." Silenced for so long by the scientific regime of Newtonian mechanics, refused by a political structure that assents only to univocal models of power, unmediated by a culture that privileges the visual sense, Hayles' theoretical imaginary does the opposite. It makes the margin the center, fluidity the essence of a new materialism, bifurcation the trigger of change, and the nonlinear—the recursive—the basis of a creative vision of "non-order" as the strange attractor of chaos. It is as if her thought presences a grand reunification of something that has not only been long refused but actually intellectually discounted—the fluctuating reality of the "far from equilibrium"—schizophrenic eye movements, fluctuations of the stock market, traffic flows, crowds, waves, clouds, and vortices.

Not simply "normal science," chaotics is also normal life. Continuously looped and relooped by the intense media significations of advanced capitalism, posthuman subjects are destined to live in complex information environments. Here electronic textuality denotes the fate of bodies as much as the futuristic configuration of new media books. At the level of individual autobiography, posthuman subjects recognize that the most dramatic of life changes often begin with minute fluctuations; that bifurcation is how lives suddenly alter; that the *clinamen*—Lucretius' "swerve"—is always present; and that for every entropic tendency in patterns of energy, there is also a "dissipative structure" just waiting to self-organize, to begin things anew. Economic chaotics; political chaotics; sexual chaotics; media chaotics: these are the material horizon of the twenty-first century under the sign of the digital code.

In the introduction to her anthology, *Chaos and Order: Complex Dynamics in Literature and Science,* Hayles argues the importance of migrating beyond the binaries of order and chaos to an understanding of chaos as "non-order." About this she is adamant:

> The science of chaos draws Western assumptions about chaos into question by revealing possibilities that were suppressed when chaos was considered merely as order's opposite. It marks the validation within the Western tradition of a view of chaos that views it as non-order. In chaos theory chaos may either lead to order, as it does with self-organizing systems, or in yin/yang fashion it may have deep structures of order encoded within it.[3]

From this perspective on chaos as "non-order" everything flows: conceptualizing chaos as "extremely complex information rather than an absence of order";[4] discovering that "hidden within the unpredictability of chaotic systems are deep structures of order";[5]

situating chaos on a par "with evolution, relativity, and quantum mechanics in its impact on the culture";[6] and finally equivocating chaos with the science of complexity—"or more precisely the sciences of complexity, for fields as diverse as meteorology, irreversible thermodynamics, epidemiology, and nonlinear dynamics are included within this rubric. The kind of systems to which chaos models have been successfully applied range from dripping faucets to measles epidemics, schizophrenic eye movements to fluctuations in fish populations."[7]

Once the thread of chaos is pulled, there can be no going back—certainly not to Newtonian mechanics, concerning which Hayles' critique is as severe as it is definitive. More than is customary, Hayles does not stop with simply distinguishing the mechanical from the fluid but uses her critique of Newtonian physics as a way of accelerating the rate of speed of chaos theory. If Newtonian mechanics and Euclidean geometry are "scale-irrelevant," then chaotics "takes scale into account," thereby acknowledging that "changes of configurations change dimensions—are complex and unpredictable."[8] To the "predictability" of Newtonian physics, chaotics is deemed unpredictable, fluid, replete with "strange attractors" (whereby "patterns combine with unpredictability, confinement with orbits that never repeat themselves"[9]) and "recursive symmetry" ("a figure or a system displays recursive symmetry when the same general form is repeated across many different length scales, as though the form were being progressively enlarged or diminished"[10]). To the world of the Newtonian clock, "chaotics focuses on the waterfall—turbulent, unpredictable, irregular, and infinitely varying in length."[11]

> The world as chaotics envisions it, then, is rich in unpredictable evolutions, full of complex forms and turbulent flows, characterized by nonlinear relations between causes and effects, and fractured into multiple-length scales that make globalization precarious.[12]

However, if Hayles can so succinctly distinguish the key differences between Newtonian mechanics and chaotics, perhaps it is because there are only *apparent* distinctions between them. In a case of theory imitating its own generative models, chaotics may well represent the "strange attractor" of Newtonian mechanics and Euclidean geometry as much as the clocklike, predictable world of Newtonian physics constitutes the hidden structure of order—the "recursive symmetry"—at the (fluctuating) heart of chaotics. If this is the case, it would mean that the choice of chaotics is always compromised by the seduction of hauntology. Consequently, migrating from physics to biology, from the clock to the waterfall, may represent in the end something more paradoxical than boundary shifting, namely, that the science of chaotics is precisely the (epistemological) negation that confirms the ineluctable presence of order as the essence of complexity. In this case, sweeping aside the Newtonian epistēmē only deepens the grip of the special problem of order on chaotics. Perhaps it is not so much chaos envisioned as non-order, but chaos and order as *twisted strands,* weaving together but pulling in opposite directions, haunting one another, seducing the other by the specter of its always missing term. In this instance, then, the study of chaotics first, and complexity later, assumes a prior importance not so much as a spectacular and decisive break with the nature of (ordered) things but as creative disturbances that are simultaneously both immanent to and yet at one remove from the real logic of power.

The Complexity Trilogy

Hayles' important trilogy—*How We Became Posthuman, My Mother Was a Computer,* and *Writing Machines*—represents, when taken together, a powerful mythopoetic vision of the posthuman subject: its informational context (chaotics); its privileged discourse (new media analysis); its evolutionary principle (complexity); and its dominant aesthetic value (intermediation). With these writings, the posthuman body begins to speak the language of twenty-first-century cybernetics; to migrate from one (electronic) medium to another (intertextuality); to differentiate digital texts from print; and to recognize that "human consciousness is computational." Beyond their specific significance as creative, detailed analyses of the impact of computation on embodiment, subjectivity, literature, and society, what might be described as the "complexity trilogy" constitutes the coming of age of posthuman subjectivity as the representative consciousness of digital reality. Running parallel to the great scientific discoveries of its times, posthuman subjectivity is fully configured within the technological envelope of advanced computation. Visualized as an "information pattern,"[13] the post-human body emerges directly from the elementary materiality of chaotics: its consciousness "probabilistic"; its mind a matter of "distributed cognition"; its reasoning by way of "analogy"; its principle of action "self-organization"; its intelligence "emergent"; and its privileged metaphyics "pattern–randomness," not "logos–absence." In essence, *posthuman subjectivity is the ideological reflex of computation in the age of complexity.* Considered *ontologically,* it is as if complexity theory actually grew a body, extending itself into the human sensorium by means of a computational mind (made flesh) seeking to expand the transformative possibilities of digital culture. Understood *epistemologically,* posthuman subjectivity is a probability function, refusing determinism in favor of a form of consciousness operating by analogy. Viewed *socially,* posthuman subjectivity can only fully realize itself by creative strategies of intermediation, discovering how different media can finally communicate with one another. And finally, neither a constructivist nor a realist, the posthuman subject is always in active aesthetic rebellion against the binary of logos–absence, struggling instead to surface the complex materiality that is pattern–randomness.

An important clearing ground, Hayles' version of complexity theory is perhaps best understood for what it most immediately opposes, for example, not for her Hans Moravec's enthusiastic vision *(Mind's Children)* of a future driven by the dumping of human consciousness into intelligent machines. In many ways, all of Hayles' writing, with its eloquent appeal for a recovery of a deeper understanding of the complex intermediations between intelligent machines and creative consciousness, represents a sustained critical response to the (human) species subordination at the center of Moravec's vision. While Moravec writes eloquently about an increasingly robotized future dominated by our technological prodigy, Hayles' perspective retains a sense of skepticism concerning the degree to which bodies will be interpolated by machines and, conversely, intelligent machines by the human passions. It's the very same with respect to contemporary visions of an approaching technological singularity at which point all things will become fully coordinated. Definitely not a digital monist, Hayles' perspective is too embodied, distributive, indeterminate, intermediated to bound itself with this most recent version of technological utopia. In equal measure, Hayles is above all a transformative scientist, one whose commitment to knowledge discourse precludes essentially millenarian religious enthusiasm in the rhetoric of technological singularities. In addition, while certainly sensitive to the creative upsurge that is postmodernism and poststructuralism, her intellectual project can never fully embrace the postmodern vision of the death of referential logic captured in all its finality and bleakness by Baudrillard's theorisation of the "terrorism of the code." While Hayles' thought dwells deeply in the detrital remains of the terrorism of the code, particularly in its frequent recourse to chillingly dystopian science fiction literature, it must be said that her ontological commitment to the complex materiality of the code would never permit her to evoke codes in the language of terror. It is not so much her dismissal of postmodernism as "excess" and "fragmented" but that she approaches the study of the code with an open-systems perspective, alert both to questions of power, ideology, and acquisitive capitalism as embedded within the logic of master codes and to the transformative possibilities for intermediating anew speech, writing, and code. This is definitely not a theorist who, refusing the blandishments of technological singularity and the literal exteriorization of the imagination (consciousness dumping), is about to succumb to an apocalyptic (postmodern) image equating the "regime of computation" with the terrorism of the code.

That Hayles refuses the alternatives of a robotic utopia (Moravec) and technological cataclysm (Baudrillard) does not necessarily mean that she is the latest exponent of technological liberalism, namely, an attitude toward technology that takes its aesthetic pleasure in striking the mean between cybernetic apocalypse and bliss. It is probably more to the point that she is the creator of a mode of feminism equal to the paradoxes and perturbations of the era of computation. Not satisfied with formulations of fixed gender and sexual identity approximating the liberal subjectivity of "possessive individualism," and certainly not content with reducing questions of gender, sexuality, and embodied subjectivity to the constructivism of the age of intelligent machines, Hayles rearticulates feminism under the sign of complexity theory. Adopting Anne Balsamo's expression "my mother was a computer" as the title of one of her major books, authoring *Writing Machines* in a doubled voice, writing *How We Became Posthuman* as an extended meditation, in part, on the question of reflexivity in relationship to embodied subjectivity, Hayles promotes a form of *enabled feminism* in the age of complexity. Intentionally, or not very much in the tradition of new French feminism, with its insistence of literally writing a woman's body into existence—a body which is authored less hierarchically than by labored scribbles, broken margins, repressed silences, a scream for social recognition that will be heard and, finally, embodied—Hayles finds the possible dimensions of a new woman's body in code. This is not an exclusively gendered woman's body, not a body within a closed loop of sexual identity, but a body nonetheless—a body of feminism, a woman's, a man's, transsexual, transgendered, artificial, maybe in the future part human, part animal, part plant—which in its "intermediations" and "recursions" and "bifurcations" and "uncertainty," is the outcome of feminist theory. Finally coming into existence in the "swerves" of complexity theory, finally finding a moment of articulation in the "emergent reality" and "dynamic hierarchies" of society under the sign of computation, this body of feminist labor, this body of feminist vision, is not about to dissolve itself in the detrital remains of technological apocalypse, singularity, or utopia. Like the emergent awareness, like the embodied subjectivity, like the complicated intermediations that are Hayles' version of feminism, this will be a body that is not reducible to uncomplicated patterns of thought or practice. Posthuman as its basic condition of possibility, a writing machine as its chosen mode of expression, and mothered into life by a computer, this feminist theory, this feminist theory of complexity, destabilizes everything—not just Judith Butler's *gender trouble* or Donna Haraway's early espousal of the *cyber* but something more indeterminate, more ontologically undermining. Not gendered in a bubble, Hayles' embodied subjectivity only exists to the extent that it is in creative tension with intelligent machines:

> Encountering intelligent machines from this perspective enables me to see that they are neither objects to dominate nor subjects threatening to dominate me. Rather, they are embodied entities instantiating processes that interact with the processes that I instantiate as an embodied human subject. The experience of interacting with them changes me incrementally, so the person who emerges from the encounter is not exactly the same person who began it.[14]

And that's the point. Like an epochal rupture with Francis Bacon's justification in *Novum Organuum* for the domination of nature, Hayles rewrites science under the sign of a different ontology—a feminist ontology—which in its foundations and prescriptions dares to think the future of a universe coded by care, characterized by entanglements, saturated with complexity, typified by "mutuality," and driven by "complex dynamics":[15]

> Disrupting the standard story of scientific realism, the computational processes that create and implement this agency have the potential to inspire another kind of narrative in which humans are not seen as subjects manipulating objects in the world.[16]
>
> In these stories, human action and agency are understood as embodied processes sharing important characteristics with the processes taking place within computational media, including possibilities for evolution and emergence.[17]

What might be called "complexity feminism" is just like that. Refusing to take its place on the margins of science and technology, it owes its very expression to a fundamental paradigmatic shift in the nature of scientific realism today. When the world is code, when intelligent machines rise beyond speech and writing to take their place in the new (cybernetic) order of things, suddenly something most unlikely, definitely unforeseen, happens—complexity feminism, the name that might be given to a possible new form of social relationships enabled by advanced computation. If the era of computation does not end with the univocal power of the "Universal Computer," then not subjectively, but objectively, a new order of complex social relationships is made possible. While Hayles will provide a wonderful vocabulary to describe these newly emergent social relationships—"reflexivity," "new materialism," "complex dynamics," "multi-causal, multi-layered"—what she is really expressing is a fundamentally new comportment toward technology, a perspective on technology owing everything to the continuing feminist rebellion out of which it has emerged and of which it represents its leading edge. Not overtly, of course, and definitely not foregrounded, the question of feminism in Hayles' theory is more subtle and consequently more constitutive. In the same way as the silent language of codes provides the establishing framework for computational culture, what might be described as a *computationally enabled feminism* exists as the basic condition of possibility of her thought. It's everywhere: the refusal of impervious boundaries; the affirmation of "emergence"; the recognition of other life-forms—artificial life, clones, hybrids; the articulation of complex human–machine entanglements; the rejection of hierarchical structures in favor of socially complicated dynamics; the language of bodies as sites of multiplicity, mutuality, and intermediation.

In a paradoxical twist of history, it's as if two powerful streams of thought—one scientific, the other feminist—have suddenly converged in complexity theory, culminating not in a familiar vision of science or feminism as we have known it but in a co-evolution and co-emergence of both terms. Here the scientific imagination is almost forcibly turned away from its modernist foundations in predatory ontologies of acquisition, control, and manipulation, becoming instead something transformative—inherently complex and potentially a process of intermediation. And feminism? When the term sinks beneath the surface of gender identity and sexual difference to become the enabling framework of a new way of understanding the complexities of subjectivity in the era of intelligent machines, it, too, is transformative, refusing its earlier affirmation of essentialist identity in favor of knowledge of complexity—complex identities, sexualities, genders, imaginations, relationships, and bodies.

As Heidegger noted long ago in "The Question Concerning Technology," the language of "enframing" is everything. Ironically, while Heidegger was reflecting directly on the languages of technological objectification—"standing-reserve," "alienation," and "harvesting"—as the invisible framework of scientifically driven nihilism, he always alluded in his thought to the future possibility of a creatively transformative logic emergent directly from science and technology. It is the modest proposal of this essay that the creative "transformation" prophesied by Heidegger—this doubled "turning" of nihilism toward objectifying both power and social creativity simultaneously—finds its twenty-first-century expression in this wonderful trilogy of books mixing avowal and skepticism, constructivism and realism as ways of imagining that other world of incommensurability, intermediation, and complexity that is *My Mother Was a Computer, Writing Machines,* and *How We Became Posthuman.*

The Posthuman Subject

Ethics of Complexity

Hayles can develop such a comprehensive critique of clashing perspectives on science and technology because her own perspective is driven by a powerful ethical vision—an ethics of complexity. Immanent to the history of wired culture out of which it emerges, her perspective absorbs the most advanced conceptual categories of information culture as the basis of ethical complexity: its object, the "Regime of Computation"; its content, "reflexivity"; its method, "intermediation"; its practice, "new materialism"; and its overarching goal, a "fluid negotiation of the multi-causal, multi-layered world of computation." Faithful to her continuing refusal of ontological binaries, this ethics of complexity is always a matter of recursive looping and a multiplicity of entanglements. Here ethics is not articulated from outside, somehow exterior to and at one remove from the scientific enterprise, but like the Heideggerian "turning" to which it bears a remarkable resemblance, the ethics of complexity represents the moment of the uncanny, the intermediation, the incommensurable in the scientific epistēmē. This is why each of her books is such a lively carnival of unlikely juxtapositions: apocalyptic science fiction authors and earnest theorists of artificial intelligence; French poststructuralists (de Saussure to Derrida) and American code makers; visions of prosthetic bodies and images of creative flows of information; the "Universal Computer" and *Patchwork Girl*; cellular automata and the fascinating literary chaotics of *House of Leaves*. A student of science, literature, chaotics, complexity, and the history and politics of life itself, Hayles actually puts into practice a strategy of *détournement*—literally turning the generative terms of the "new science" from the inside, following the twisted strands of cellular automata, computation, reflexivity, intertextuality, intermediation, new materialism, and new media analysis until they are, finally, forced to disclose their possibilities for "multi-causal, multi-layered analysis."

Very much in the tradition of technological humanism first so eloquently expressed in the writings of Marshall McLuhan, Hayles' ethics of complexity finds itself in the computational storm center of the new science of artificial emergence. But whereas McLuhan's Roman Catholic humanism influences his thought in the ethically deductive direction of the *ratio dicendum* of the great medieval theologians, Thomas Aquinas most of all, Hayles does something very different. McLuhan's mind worked aphoristically, throwing out word probes as ways of disturbing the electromagnetic field of communication technologies as it silently massaged the human sensorium into submission; Hayles' ethics works analogically, creating unlikely juxtapositions to reveal the uncanny in the regime of computation. But for all that, Hayles and McLuhan share a common ethical vector, both deeply motivated by the passivity with which contemporary culture accepts the mind-dumping logic of intelligent machines running on AI software; both opposed to the artificial separation of science and the humanities; both studying intently the myths, logic, strategies, and tactics of advanced science for clues to collective survival strategies; and both absorbing, poetically and scientifically, the language of science as a way of making that which would be technologically self-referential a form of reflexivity that would be creatively emergent.

Nowhere is the ethics of complexity more persuasively demonstrated than in the pages of *My Mother Was a Computer*. Perhaps mindful of McLuhan's insight that technology now functions most powerfully, and insidiously, as an invisible medium, this book adopts a literary strategy once proposed by the French theorist of mythologies, Roland Barthes, of using theory and literature and creative thought itself as iron filings thrown across the invisible field of the regime of computation so as to reveal its multiple dimensions, its hybrid layers. As a code breaker, the structure of the text is perfect. It presents itself as a literary simulacrum of the era of computation: "Making: Language and Code," "Storing: Print and Text," and "Transmitting: Analog and Digital." Formally, the text is a straightforward version of the organizing logic of the data archive with the interface ("transmitting") front-loaded, memory archiving ("storing") at the back end, and computational transcription ("making") as the actual operating code. Literally, it is no exaggeration to state that the mother of this book is a computer. Theoretically recursive of the logic of computation, the very structure of the text is the invisible medium of the computer itself, with the argument of the text shaped, influenced, and channeled by this projection of the threefold logic of computer-mediated society into a powerful literary form. When the data archive comes alive, when computer-mediated culture reveals itself in all its complexity in *My Mother Was a Computer,* then we know that we are in the presence, not of an ethical critique somehow distanced from the data archive, but of an expression of ethics directly proximate to the language of data. When data speaks, when my (literary) mother is computation, when the archive is populated with novels and stories (Neil Stephenson's *Cryptomicon,* Stanislaw Lem's "The Mask," Shelley Jackson's *Patchwork Girl*), with media ("Speech, Writing, Code: Three Worldviews"), with science ("Intermediation: Textuality and the Regime of Computation"), with unknown relatives ("Computing Kin"), with futurist prophecy ("Recursion and Emergence"), then we must finally acknowledge that what has been *presenced* is an ethics of complexity that is true to its (data) word, namely, that reading this text, scanning this text, will take us into the data archive of our own subjectivity in an epoch of computation. If this is the case, if subjectivity today, computer-mediated subjectivity, has itself been rendered into an invisible medium of the greater power of computation—its memory back-ended and archived; its practices electronically flexible and increasingly technically operational; its interfaces, bodies and skin and facial expressions as screensavers presented in real time to the world—then *My Mother Was a Computer* is really not so much a cultural study of new science as the first and, perhaps, best of all the individual autobiographies of digital subjectivity. In this book, the digital subjects that we have (increasingly) become experience something of a homecoming as the thread of missing computer kin, cellular automata, intelligent machines, and prosthetic culture leads to its terminus ad quem, namely, ourselves as the elementary subjective particles of computer-enabled society.

By extension, the strategy of computational mimesis by which Hayles evokes the logic of the code as the silent medium of her writings expands to the complexity trilogy as a whole. Viewed as a data archive of posthuman subjectivity, the three interrelated books in the complexity trilogy represent a seamless cybernetic architecture: the history of contemporary computing—*How We Became Posthuman*—as the back-end memory archive; the reflexive literary interface of *Writing Machines* as a material analysis of the new media within which we are inscribed; and the complexity theorems of *My Mother Was a Computer* as the operating code of the (computational) system as a whole. Entering posthuman subjectivity as writing machines, either passively inscribed or actively recoding, our choice is to be either passively drawn along in the powerful stream of emergent cellular automata or active, self-reflexive minds and bodies fully attentive to the doubled challenge that is *My Mother Was a Computer,* looking for guidance about the future to the tutor text of *How We Became Posthuman.*

There are strange loops here, multiple recursions, creative opportunities for twisting together genealogy, ethics, and practice, "minute deviations" that suddenly amplify into widespread cultural shifts, clashing perspectives that refuse to be binary opponents, folding instead into a beautiful field of instability, impurity, and (digital) unorthodoxies. Computational culture has finally found a way of going beyond the necessary silence of the codes, instituting a heuristic practice in the pages of the complexity trilogy, which has the most unusual effect of reconfiguring thought itself as a form of computer-mimesis. If, for Hayles, the mind is not to be passively dumped into the data bins of intelligent machines, then it must reconfigure consciousness—creatively recode the digital brain—as a survival strategy for understanding the full social impact of computational culture: (data) archive, (complex) logic, and (creative) interface, therefore, as the trinitarian logic of posthuman subjectivity, the once and only real opposition to the technological deterministic vision of *ourselves* as evolutionary appendages to the Universal Computer.

In the eloquent epilogue ("Recursion and Emergence") to *My Mother Was a Computer,* Hayles is clear about her larger intentions:

> The crucial question with which this book has been concerned is how the "new kind of science" that underwrites the Regime of Computation can serve to deepen our understanding of what it means to be in the world rather than apart from it, co-maker rather than dominator, participants in the complex dynamics that connect "what we make" and "what (we think) we are." Amid the uncertainties, potentialities, and dangers created by the Regime of Computation, simulations—computational and narrative—can serve as potent resources with which to explore and understand the entanglement of language with code, the traditional medium of print with electronic textuality, and subjectivity with computation.[18]

This is exactly what *My Mother Was a Computer* does. Beginning with its initial critique of the inadequacies inherent in both constructivism (computation as a metaphor) and realism (computation as an emergent reality) and continuing with its exploration of the earth, sky, and water of speech, writing, and codes, Hayles "drives," in her description, complexity theory "into the neocortex" of literary theory specifically and liberal subjectivity more generally. Methodologically, her entanglement with questions of constructivism and realism replicates long-standing philosophical concern with the nature of reality itself and the role of consciousness within it. Beyond the scientific epistēmē, this debate has found its most intense philosophical expression in the writings of Martin Heidegger's *Identity and Difference.* In the latter, Heidegger stressed the question of identity to the point of "oblivion," precisely that moment when a possible language of difference emerges that is simultaneously fully proximate to identity and its impossible other. Could it be that the terms *computation-as-metaphor* and *reality-principle* can be so immediately unsettling for Hayles because, in a way that is similar to the pathways traced by *Identity and Difference,* her thought is an enduring quest not only to understand the "ground" of computational being but also to draw out from the shadows the specter of difference? Consider Heidegger's fateful words:

> One comes over the other, one arrives in the other. Overwhelming and arrival appear in each other in reciprocal reflection. Speaking in terms of difference, this means: perdurance is a circling, the circling of Being and beings around each other.[19]

Could there be a more eloquent, succinct description of complexity theory in relationship to (computational) ontology and emergence than "one comes over the other, one arrives in the other"? Thought metaphysically, *My Mother Was a Computer* identifies the historical grounding of contemporary being—the "Regime of Computation"—but also traces that which is grounded, namely, ourselves as posthuman subjects. As metaphor, computation remains for Hayles a "useful heuristic" but not a decisive challenge to such issues as embodiment, subjectivity, and identity. As an emergent reality-principle, computation suddenly aspires to the higher status of cosmology, becoming a generative reality machine in its own right, with its own patterns of ontology, epistemology, axiology, and aesthetics. Like Heidegger before her, Hayles refuses to privilege either interpretation to the exclusion of its opposite, preferring a form of thought similar to "perdurance," that moment when, in the folded twists of complexity theory, "one comes over the other, one arrives in the other."

Consequently, what are the different chapters in this book—Hayles' brilliant reinscription of Derrida's "logos–absence" and de Saussure's formal semiology as necessary, but insufficient, conditions for discovering the "locus of complexity"; her meditations on "performative code and figurative language"; or the choice of Stanislaw Lem's "The Mask" as a tutor text for understanding "subjective cosmology and the regime of computation"—but ways of opening up posthuman subjectivity to Heidegger's prophecy: "overwhelming and arrival appear in each other in reciprocal reflection"? Whether in the ancient languages of the gods or the contemporary codes of computation, one thing is certain: the question of Being has not disappeared, and with it the problematic relationship of identity and difference is no less muted for its necessary expression in the vocabulary of a culture all the more profoundly religious for its computational aspirations. Is not complexity theory a form of "perdurance," a constant "overwhelming and arrival [that] appear in each other in reciprocal reflection"? And if this is so, might it not be said that the ethics of complexity is actually a heuristic of the main propositions of Heidegger's *Identity and Difference*—a literary and scientific "perdurance" that represents "the circling of Being and beings around each other."

And there is something else: faithful to Hayles' example of deploying tutor texts as ways of understanding differences in texts, media, and art, what would happen if *Identity and Difference* was to be used as a tutor text for approaching *My Mother Was a Computer*? This choice follows from the ethics of complexity, which privileges the engagement of the uncanny. Certainly there is no deep affiliation of literary practices or philosophical perspectives between the texts. Heidegger the metaphysician (of completed nihilism) and Hayles the theorist (of complexity) circle around one another in a noisy silence, their approaches to the question of technology dramatically different in every respect: methodologically, aesthetically, practically. Indeed, with her emphasis on the interruptions, the caesura of (computational) being, it might be said that Hayles continues the tradition of postmetaphysical thought in which, as Heidegger has noted, the question of Being retreats into the shadows of the gods. Yet there is for all the obvious differences between Hayles and Heidegger the stubborn, inconvertible fact that there between them is a question of *difference,* and that difference, that question of what is between Hayles and Heidegger, may well represent a decisive expression of "overwhelming and arrival" in the regime of computation. By stepping back into this difference, we might well be stepping forward into a deeper understanding of the issues at stake in the ethics of complexity.

Concerning the metaphysical dominance of the technological project, Heidegger is adamant:

> Let us at long last stop conceiving technology as something purely technical, that is, in terms of man and his machines. Let us listen to the claim placed in our age not only upon man, but also upon all beings, nature and history with regard to their Being.[20]

Unlike Heidegger's recurrence to the fragments of Parmenides as a means of thinking identity as "sameness," there is nothing self-evidently metaphysical about Hayles' thought. But while fully absorbed in the vicissitudes of computational experience, her mind, for all that, touches deeply on technology as metaphysics. Heidegger remarked that technology is now the essence of Being, with this equivocation: "Precisely because this entry requires a spring, it must take its time, the time of thinking which is different from the time of calculation that pulls our thinking in all directions. Today, the computer calculates thousands of relationships in one second. Despite their technical uses, they are inessential."[21] Refusing the "time of calculation," and immensely suspicious of the hegemonic claims of technological sameness, Hayles' arguments draw close to the "entry" to the question of technology. After all, just as much as *How We Became Postmodern* began with a repudiation of Moravec's image of mind harvesting by intelligent machines, *My Mother Was a Computer* is based equally on an immediate dissent against Stephen Wolfram's *A New Kind of Science*:

> The third claim, often not stated explicitly, is implied by the sweeping consequences Wolfram envisions for his research. This is the strong claim that computation does not merely simulate the behavior of complex systems; computation is envisioned as the process that generates behavior in everything from biological organisms to human social systems.[22]

More than an exclusively scientific debate concerning the ability of computation to actually "generate reality," Hayles' ethics of complexity pulls apart from the regime of computation to approach it even closer. Here (technological) identity and (complex) difference circle one another, representing simultaneously an "overwhelming" (the "regime of computation") and an "arrival" ("complex dynamics"), or, in Heidegger's terms, "a thinking forward, which is not a planning."[23] While there is definitely not a linear correspondence between Hayles and Heidegger, there is still a sense in brushing *Identity and Difference* against *My Mother Was a Computer* that some essential intellectual spark in the "house of being" has passed between them intertextually—that somehow, inadvertently perhaps, a long-silenced meditation by Heidegger on the recovery of the act of thinking as "appropriation" has somehow infiltrated the framing of *My Mother Was a Computer*. That *My Mother Was a Computer* represents, both in its specifics and its entirety, an extended meditation on the house of (technological) being, a "thinking forward" that has about it the "event of appropriation":

> But this abyss is neither empty nothingness nor murky confusion; but rather: the event of appropriation. In the event of appropriation vibrates the active nature of what speaks as language, which at one time was called the house of Being.[24]

In this case, it is not the preeminent media of speech and writing but *code* that is the "event of appropriation," the careful study of which takes us deeply into the "house of (technological) being." As *My Mother Was a Computer* argues in magnificent detail, there is real trouble in the house of (technological) being—trouble not only from increasingly frequent manifestations of technological enthusiasm motivated by reducing codework to a conversionary experience in data mining the recesses of human subjectivity but, more to the point, extreme trouble with eloquently argued accounts, both literary and scientific, of a "new science" of computation as an emergent reality in and of itself. Presented scientifically by Wolfram's *A New Kind of Science* and profoundly more ambivalently, in literary fiction, by Greg Egan's *Permutation City* and *Quarantine,* the vision of reality itself as both generated and programmed by the Universal Computer realizes the most dystopian moment of the electronic simulacrum as exteriorizing the human sensorium. Here struggles in the house of (technological) being between identity and difference are resolved in favor of a seductive image of computation as a generative reality in its own right. When the logic of cellular automata goes postbiological, when cybernetic reflexivity mutates in the direction of emergence, computation ceases to be merely mathematical. It migrates instead to the language of postbiological evolutionism. Definitely not a language of technological domination, the vision of computation as a generative reality nominates itself in the name of life, specifically artificial life and artificial intelligence. Inaugurated by a decisive species break, evolving beyond the human, beyond nature, code as a generative reality is a transcendental signifier on its way to the age of intelligent machines.

Everything in *My Mother Was a Computer* passionately and articulately struggles against code as a transcendental signifier; everything in this text refuses to subsume reality in the identity of the Universal Computer, arguing instead for a renewal, a complex renewal, of an embodied tension between identity and difference. That's why the text can be so excessively, so luxuriantly metaphysical. Not having to travel (digitally) very far, it discovers the essence of technology close at home. What do we have here but a twenty-first-century case study application of *Identity and Difference*: an "event of appropriation" that, sweeping across the cultural vistas of speech, writing, and code, here evoking the most chilling of science fiction apocalyptic visions, there brilliantly vivisecting theoretical arguments in support of code as ontology, now studying the "knotty oxymorons" of exhausted dialectics, later hinting at radically new conceptualizations of intertextuality, represents a recovery of the forgotten language of "overwhelming" and "arrival." To the *overwhelming* of code as ontology, Hayles responds with a series of *code arrivals*: the arrival of complexity theory; the arrival of a form of (computational) emergence that would not be transcendental; the arrival of code that loops from the smoothness of recursive symmetry to the "unruliness," "multiplicity," and "messiness" of embodiment; the arrival, in short, of an idea of textuality that is "instantiated rather than dematerialized, dispersed rather than unitary, processual rather than object-like, flickering rather than durably imprinted."[25] If the language of code is how (technological) being speaks to us today, then the analysis of *My Mother Was a Computer* vibrates at the recursive edge of emergence and immersion, externalization (of the human nervous system) and intermediation, binary codes spoken by machines and native languages conversant with the (human) ear.

We might well be living in the practical realization of the "dream of information," but Hayles' "event of appropriation" reveals something of the truth of that dream in all its bliss and terror. From its analysis of "software as ideology" and its critique of "predatory capitalism" to its understanding of code as "transubstantiation," as "reinscription," as "re-incarnation," *My Mother Was a Computer* reveals an empire of code that frames the evolving, seemingly postbiological story of (technological) being within traces of seduction and deprival.

The Practice of Complexity

It is the very same with *Writing Machines.* Ostensibly a study of "media and materiality," this book represents in its design and (digital) literariness the practice of complexity today.

Again the antecedent for the design element of this project is Marshall McLuhan's *The Medium Is the Massage,* with its blown-up pages, distorted typefaces, wired aphorisms, and liquid writing. Frustrated with the imprisonment of writing within the invisible medium of the printed page, McLuhan became the first and best of all the visual deconstructionists, making of *The Medium Is the Massage* a book in which reading (and the reader) take a bath. With its electrical storm of aphorisms and its hard-track demolition of the symmetry of the printed word, McLuhan's imagination launched the practice of complexity. However, that said, it is the significant contribution of *Writing Machines* to do McLuhan one better, not only visually deconstructing print design but actually traveling deeply into the physical materiality of writing machines, those great contemporary works of electronic literature—*House of Leaves, A Humament, Lexia to Perplexia*—that capture the complex dynamics that is digital literacy today. With *Writing Machines,* electronic literature is finally recognized less as an evolutionary step beyond the age of print than as something more intermediated, materialist, and, ironically, physical, namely, a complexity literature.

The writing machine that is electronic literature knows this about the world. It knows that speech and writing are entangled with the newly insurgent language of code. It knows that code is a literature with its own internal rules of symmetry, signification, and recursion. It knows that code, like life itself, loops and reloops, travels at light speed, warp-holes through the unitary fabric of space-time, yet also circulates deeply in the physical materiality of bodies, subjectivity, and the printed page. It knows that code has its ideological limitations, that code is always framed by the binaries of 1 and 0, that code is strictly performative, that code is limited to the executable, and that, consequently, code must be performance driven or die. And finally, it knows that code, like the astronomical journeys of the stars before (and after) it, may well, in fact, sweep by this planet of earth, sky, water, and air at escape velocity but, for all that, cannot itself escape being influenced by the ecstasy and melancholy of the human condition. Terrorized by the imperative of executable code, the language of code is a natural AI schizoid—its very (performative) life is dependent on the executability, the operationality of its functions, but its fate tends to melancholy. Unlike its cultural companions—speech and writing—both of which accompany their actual performances in orality and literature with imaginary silences, code can never have about it the necessary reserve of silence, can never seek to undo its limits of "executability" by making of itself its own undoing. Consequently, while speech may culminate in the excesses of Babylon and writing in the delirium of the printed word, the machinery of code knows only one inevitable end—the (computational) culture of profound boredom. Which is why perhaps another theoretical analyst of codework, Jean Baudrillard, can so evocatively and powerfully conjure up the language of the "terrorism of the code" as that which is simultaneously most fearful about computation and yet most desired by the language of code itself. It turns out that like speech and writing before it, code revels in its own approaching apocalypse, is animated by the merest hint of catastrophe, is seduced by traces of negation that threaten to undo the regime of "executable code."

Confronted with these enigmas inherent in the era of computation, Hayles splits in two, actually becoming a bifurcated subject, a literary schizoid, to capture something of the complex dynamics of contemporary electronic literature. Spinning off a literary double named Kaye ("no one should confuse her with me"[26]), Hayles adopts the complex writing strategy of the uncanny code. At the strictly theoretical level, she remains the primary author, introducing distinctions between simulation and materiality, calling attention to the necessity for a new "new ecology," and clarifying the importance of the concept of "remediation" as a way of understanding the entangled relationship of print and digitality. Kaye is very different. She is constructed with an interesting life history originating in the American Midwest, loves books of all kinds, receives an advanced education in science and the humanities, and enjoys that most floating of all experiences: she is simultaneously attracted to the experimental precision of science while all the while being seduced by the literary abject. An early practitioner of the digital way, Kaye experiences her (technological) epiphany in the now rustic form of a desktop computer:

> When she first encountered the desktop computer and realized that it could be used to create literary texts, she realized that everything important to her met in the nexus of this material-semiotic object. It called forth the questions that continued to fascinate her about scientific research: what does it mean? Why is it important? It confronted her with the materiality of the physical world and its mediation through the technological apparatus.[27]

But what Kaye doesn't realize is that the technological apparatus is about to run right over her autobiography: first, in the language of (scientific) simulations, which, once the generative reality program is running, seem to suddenly expand everywhere into the flesh and blood of the world conceived as hyperspace, and, second, in the form of postmodern (Baudrillardian) theory—Kaye's particular bête noire—which seizes on the triumph of computation to construct a vision of fourth-order simulation wherein modernist divisions between simulation and materiality are erased under the ecstatic sign of the "disappearance of the real." Ultimately more a late modernist than a postmodernist, committed to an expansion of liberal subjectivity in the direction of complexity theory, always seeking to rework the binaries of simulation and materiality in the fluid language of identity and difference, Kaye remains a polite, but fierce, opponent of the singularity of hypersimulation—perhaps it was her background as a child in northeastern Missouri three hours' drive "along limestone bluffs to the Hannibal of Mark Twain fame"; perhaps it was the simple fact that her hometown of Clarence was cut in half by the speeding trains of the Union Pacific Railroad, that she may have grown up on the prairies but technology had made of her home a test bed crash site; or perhaps it was those twists of a restless mind oscillating between the dreams of scientific clarity and the interpretative pleasure of the literary text. Whatever the reason, whatever the founding passion, Kaye was born to complexity theory by virtue of her physical and intellectual autobiographies. By a deep epistemological preference formed first along those "limestone cliffs" and confirmed by the intermediation of that speeding train running through her hometown, Kaye could never be either postmodern or a traditional modernist. The skepticism of Mark Twain provides the first clue. Against the apocalyptic visions of postmodernism, she remembers too well those other forgotten materialities—embodiment, subjectivity, circulating bodies, restless imaginations. And, beyond modernism, she recognizes early that it is far too late to recover the honor of the great, now superseded referentials of the humanities without reference to complex media ecologies that trace the unfolding history of simulation and materiality. This is why Kaye recognizes in the hapless object of the desktop computer a "material-semiotic" object, which, if stressed, will propel her along the byways of the "dream of information." It is also why her double in real life, Katherine Hayles, can translate the complexity that is her mind with all its bifurcations, remediations, minute deviations, and traces of allegorical ellipsis into the actual practice of complexity that is *Writing Machines*. Like a beautiful mise-en-scène, the actual object of *Writing Machines* may be the collapse of borders between simulation and materiality in the real-time world of electronic literature, but its actual contribution is the doubled autobiography of complexity theory itself.

The Genealogy of Complexity

If *Writing Machines* is about material practices and *My Mother Was a Computer* focuses on simulation, then *How We Became Posthuman: Virtual Bodies in Cybernetics, Literature, and Informatics* is their brilliant mediation, that moment where the vectors traced by these books are actually anticipated and converge in advance. Here we move beyond scenes of bodily slippages, exclusions, and hybridities to the *posthuman* reality of complex bodies, where "information has lost its body" but the body itself, with its memories, traces, desires, and history, has, and will never lose, its sense of embodiment. Now that we find ourselves located in technological subjectivity, what are its possibilities for transformation or disappearance? Refusing to look away from the (distributed) reality of cybernetics, Hayles does the opposite. She forces the history of cybernetics to reveal its secret. In an increasingly processed culture where we find ourselves circulating like data trash within cybernetic loops of displaced meaning, where the media phantasmagoria of celebrities, diets, panic disorders, pandemics, and ceaseless rumors circulates within and through bodily textuality, how do we learn to gesture to the new spaces and times of complexity? How do we actually learn to crack the shell of bounded liberal subjectivity, becoming the posthuman subjects that are simultaneously the end and means of complexity theory itself? Closed cybernetic loops. Self-reflexive loops. Emergent bodies. How really did information lose its body? And how can the complexity of information finally be recorporealized, refusing the seductive but deterministic language of transcendental singularities in favor of embodied subjectivity? As Hayles argues, "just because information has lost its body does not mean that humans and the world have lost theirs."[28]

Very much in the tradition of Michel Foucault's patient deconstruction of the gray matter of genealogy, Hayles deconstructs the history of computation. In her writings, we are imaginatively present in the first wave of cybernetics, from the famously multidisciplinary Macy Conferences on Cybernetics to the "cybernetic anxiety" of Norbert Weiner. Here, stripped of the language of embodiment, information under the sign of cybernetics begins to circulate in purely symbolic form—codework moving in closed loops seemingly emancipated from its surrounding social condition comprising questions of race, class, sexuality, and gender. While certainly not noted by Hayles, it is also as if we are present at a fantastic replay of the originary language of Augustinian Christianity itself, with the purely symbolic language of grace circulating across the surface of souls that have lost their bodies. In each case, an almost extraterrestrial universe opens up—self-sufficient, circulating, mapping—that is at one dramatic remove from the complexity, the intermediations, of embodied subjectivity. It's the very same in terms of the "second wave of cybernetics," which, rebelling against the closed information loops of primitive cybernetics, literally turns reality inside out, moving from "reflexivity to self-organization," from the "hyphen to the splice." Everything is here: the fiction of Phillip K. Dick; the "autopoietic machines" of Humberto Maturana and Francisco Varela; the ascent of information from the programmed world of cybernetic feedback to a generative, evolutionary reality in its own right. To read these pages is to be relocated at the boundary between autopoiesis and reflexivity, that rupture where information under the poetic pressure of autopoiesis threatens to become a closed system, "leaving historical contingency on the outside"[29] and reflexivity, with its "embodied minds," moving at the speed of light. "No longer Wiener's island of life in a sea of entropy or Maturana's autonomous circularity, awareness realized itself as a part of a larger whole—unbounded, empty, serene."[30]

If Hayles can be eloquent in her deconstruction of the regime of computation, it is because there is something larger at stake in this book—not merely a cultural history of informational insurgency but something simultaneously unbounded and bounded in Hayles' perspective on the body. First and foremost, the question of cybernetics, whether first wave or second wave, is deeply entangled with bounded liberal subjectivity. For Hayles, cybernetics emerges as an ideological reflex of classical liberal subjectivity with its fixed borders, contained self, and necessarily stipulated spaces between all the binaries: nature–culture, subject–object, body–technology. That this is a bounded world is evidenced as much by Norbert Wiener's growing realization that humans are fated to be "cogs" within the dense matrix of cybernetic loops of information feedback as it is by Hans Moravec's ecstatic vision of ourselves as "mind's children." Indeed, for Hayles, the problem of cybernetic determination goes one step further, reflecting not simply our passive integration into the data stream but also the fact that the liberal subject is sequestered within a metaphysics of presence–absence:

> When the self is seen as grounded in presence, identified with originary guarantees and teleological trajectories, associated with solid foundations and logical trajectories, the posthuman is likely to be seen as antihuman because it assumes a conscious mind running as a small subsystem of self-construction and self-coherence while ignorant of the complexities of the larger world.[31]

And that's the point. Immediately presenting the challenge to received interpretations of the liberal subject ("What is lethal is grafting the posthuman onto the liberal humanist view of the self"[32]), Hayles makes of *How We Became Posthuman* something more decisive than a genealogy of cybernetics and definitely more radical than a prolegomena to the history of the posthuman. Certainly the text is about posthumanism, and eloquently so. In a beautiful elegy for the once and future presence of the posthuman, she writes,

Emergence replaces teleology, reflexive epistemology replaces objectivism; distributed cognition replaces embodied will; embodiment replaces a view of the body as a support system for the mind; and a dynamic partnership between humans and machines replaces the liberal humanist's manifest destiny of dominating and controlling nature.[33]

But if this book were simply a literary manifesto for the emergence of unbounded posthuman subjectivity from the data files of cybernetics, modeling, and reflexivity, its intellectual fate would be that of a great discourse of mirrored repetition and reinstallation: *mirrored repetition* because the generative terms of the posthuman—bounded versus unbounded, emergence versus teleology, reflexivity versus objectivism—simply replicate in reverse order the enframing logic of the modern (liberal) subject, and a *reinstallation* because the substitution of the embodied posthuman subject for the increasingly disembodied liberal subject has the ultimate effect of simply inverting, and thus saving, the language of the (modernist) binaries that Hayles is so intent on surpassing. If this were the case, the charismatic image of posthuman subjectivity would make its very first appearance in postcybernetic history an ironic confirmation of the ineluctable presence of the binaries that it was intended to exceed.

Which is why, I believe, the importance of *How We Became Posthuman* has definitely less to do with its evocation of the term *posthuman* as a name for the contemporary historical epoch than it does a profound overcoming of posthumanism itself. While it is certainly not customary for the creators of a (posthuman) discourse to immediately act as its great wreckers, that is precisely the significance of this text. In those wonderful concluding chapters, literally a posthumanity of pages where Hayles establishes in lyrical detail the dream of the posthuman—the vision ultimately of a culture of pattern–randomness, not presence–absence—there is always the tangible sense of a difference that cannot be easily reconciled with the tidy binaries of humanism versus posthumanism. Not so much a genealogy, and definitely not a repetition, this book about posthumanism is also a eloquent tombstone to its instant disappearance. In all her searching—in the quest for "embodied actuality," in the demand for meaning from the "entanglement" of artificial life and embodied subjectivity, in the challenge to the universe for a response to questions of inscription and supplementarity and intermediation—Hayles' particular brilliance is that she is reaching for a third space, a "perdurance," a nameless coming over and crossing back, a certain uncanniness, and, why not utter it finally, a complexity, a complex human subjectivity. *How We Became Posthuman* is an elegiac monument to the lasting importance of posthumanism as an anticipatory sign of that which is always immanent in the writings of Katherine Hayles—the immediate eclipse of posthuman subjectivity as the sun begins to rise on *complexity* as the creative subjectivity and inscribed objectivity that is the real destiny of *My Mother Was a Computer, Writing Machines,* and *How We Became Posthuman.* In the very best of the tradition of critical intellectuality, Katherine Hayles is her own undoing, making of the posthuman a sign for that which always must remain unsaid: complexity as perdurance, complexity as the completed metaphysics of an era that increasingly wagers its very being on the question of computation.

4

HYBRIDITIES: DONNA HARAWAY AND BODIES OF PARADOX

There is a painting by the Canadian artist Alex Colville that power-fully captures, although in reverse image, the theoretical imagina-tion of Donna Haraway. Titled *Horse and Train,* the painting regis-ters an approaching collision of two radically dissimilar forces—the mechanical technology of the speeding train running on its fixed track and the beautiful, but possibly doomed, spirit of the horse. No merger of the two is possible; their only future is either the death of the animal or, perhaps, one of them suddenly ceding place to the other: the train stops in time or the horse suddenly veers away. With this painting, we are introduced to a deeper discourse on technology as warring solitudes, with neither (technological) culture nor (animal) nature having any part of a shared destiny, unless the question of their technological future also alludes to the prospect of extinguishment.

The theoretical canvas of Donna Haraway is the very opposite of Colville's vision. Where her images of technology are as me-ticulously word-painted, from the literature of cyborgs, zombies, aliens, and misfits to the sciences of paleontology, biology, anthro-pology, and (women's) history, and her images of the companion species—dogs, horses, birds, apes, chimpanzees—which we are in theory and among which we circulate in practice are as passionately visualized as Colville's *Horse and Train,* her thought always rises to a greater sense of hybridity, to a critical understanding that out of the impossibility of this collision of horse and train might yet emerge a difference that inspires social justice. Always at the edge of her thought, yet deeply immanent within its detailed critical realism, there is that elusive presence of a third term not yet articulated, a godless cyborg not yet recognized, a primate feminism not yet theorized, an overcoming of the "onco-mouse" not yet happening, a transformative science not yet initiated.

It is not as if her writings have sought to avoid the extremes or, for that matter, suffer any particular sense of naivety about the likely irreconcilability of the hard elementary forces of nature with which they engage. More than most, her theoretical imagination paints a truly bleak, chillingly antiseptic, but, for all that, a relentlessly dynamic vision of the power of technology. Here the language of technology as (human) destiny achieves something of a reluctant scientific crescendo. Never constrained by limited vision or held back by any particular loyalty to the idea that the reality-principle of social domination should be watered down in the process of its critical discovery and diagnosis, Haraway's writings reveal the apocalypse that is possibly the contemporary end condition of hundreds of years of (Western) scientific experimentalism. Not a temporally limited set of observations, Haraway takes us back historically to the philosophical and anthropological origins of the scientific epistēmē *(Primate Visions)* and reflects on the doubled futures of hybrid bodies *(Simians, Cyborgs, and Women)* and genetically engineered human–animal–plant laboratory remixes *(Modest Witness),* all this with a steadfast commitment to the ideal of *The Companion Species Manifesto* in the context of a critical, materialist study of gender, race, culture, and class framed by the "informatics of domination." Refusing to confront the will to technology directly in terms of its own justificatory framework of understanding, Haraway always productively works the edges of dominant discourse, exploring the experimental history of paleontology and anthropology, the vivisected histories of chimpanzees and apes, questions of sexual dimorphism, the forgotten histories of storytelling, of art exhibitions, of TV programs, of scientific visions gone right, gone astray, gone mad, as ways of drawing into sharp visual relief the logic of nihilism that is at the heart of the language of science.

Not, of course, that she ever really discusses nihilism. Always the last and best representative of a truly *transformative* scientist, Haraway is a trusty guide to the study of hybrid bodies because her thought represents the self-reflexive logic of scientific cosmology generally and the vision of the biologist specifically. Reading Haraway is to migrate into the recursively looped consciousness of the scientific imaginaire, beyond the radical experiments by which natural scientists seek to make of the world a process of "ground-truthing," and even beyond the necessarily complicated reasons for the rise and fall of particular scientific epistēmēs to that fateful collision in the materiality of everyday life and death—the fluid datum of race, gender, class, sexuality—wherein (scientific) reason meets its (materially inscribed) body: the logic of horse and train, again and again. Definitely not a historian of science in the strict sense nor an aspirant to social utopia, Haraway makes of her own thought a knot of hybridities. This might explain why she can so fully, and powerfully, reveal the logic of scientific nihilism without once explicitly evoking the concept itself. Probably as a creative forerunner of an insurgent perspective struggling to be born, a perspective which thus far has gone nameless, except perhaps in the balky nomenclature of *aliberals, anormals, ahumans,* Haraway exemplifies the doubled logic at the heart of nihilism. If the image of nihilism can conjure up apocalyptic visions of a deracinating technological logic seeking to reduce nature and (social) nature to a passive instrumentality in the service of what Nietzsche alluded to as the "nothingness within," then nihilism also has an opposite, transformative dimension. This would be the singular contribution of Heidegger's Nietzsche: that nihilism is itself the essential destiny of contemporary (Western) being because there is always, and only, a space for discovering the "in-dwelling" of technology within the materiality of its most despotic moments. Which is why, I would suggest, "Haraway" is the name given today to the unfinished dialogue between Nietzsche and Heidegger—the name crafted in critical (material) scholarship out of the violence of the entanglement of science in the contemporary human condition. Ironically, it is in the eloquent sweep of Haraway's thought, this the most radically (destabilizing) feminist of feminists, the most radically (deconstructive) Marxist of Marxists, the most radically (self-reflexive) scientist of scientists, that we can finally discover something of the essential truth of the destiny that is the contemporary historical project of technology.

It is for Haraway neither a constructivism that would be fully abstracted nor a realism that would be nonrelational, but something else. Here we are finally present at the "crossing-over" that Nietzsche could only hint at, the "in-dwelling" that Heidegger could only speculate about, the "hybridities" of which so many feminist theorists, including Luce Irigaray and Hélenè Cixous, could only dream. Here we are, in fact, brought into the presence of a transformative possibility in the logic of science itself: from the brutality of the science of primates, a primate vision of the *commingling* of species, animals, discourses, feminisms, struggles against racism, colonialism, homophobia; from the seductions of the new universal language of the "genome," a multiple, diverse, *co-constituting* sense of new social communities that would not be genomic but creative *remixes* of culture and nature and humans and animals and the spirit-earth. It is always unpredictable in which thinker the spirit of the (scientific) times will find its fullest approximation and overcoming, always a matter of fate which theoretical pathway will align itself with the broader historical trajectory of the times in which we live, but I think it might be said with some confidence that, in these dark times, there is an unmistakable sign of a certain critical illumination reflected by and, in itself, carrying forward the thought of Donna Haraway. In her thought, there is an answer just waiting to be heard to the larger philosophical enigma concerning the fate of the body, identity, and ourselves in fact, namely, now that we have achieved the "universal, homogenous state" of technology that was Hegel's vision of fully realized history, is there a "difference" that would be transformative of science itself, a difference that would turn the future certainty of natural apocalypse into a greater human hope?

Science Flees the Galaxy

A recent news report from Hong Kong quoted the renowned scientist Stephen Hawking as stating that the very survival of the human race "depends on its ability to find new homes elsewhere in the universe because there's an increasing risk that a disaster will destroy the Earth":

> "It is important for the human race to spread out into space for the survival of the species," Hawking said. "Life on earth is at the ever-increasing risk of being wiped out by a disaster, such as sudden global warming, nuclear war, a genetically engineered virus or other dangers which we have not yet thought of."[1]

Mindful of the equally bleak scenario about (terminal) global climate change presented most persuasively by Al Gore in his film *An Inconvenient Truth,* Hawking's desire to recapitulate the use and abandon the philosophy of contemporary technological practice finds itself at the apex of growing scientific fascination with the possibility of extragalactic exploration for purposes of the survival of the human species. However, Hawking in particular, and the human race more generally, could save themselves from what may well be the doomed futility of massive extragalactic migration by reflecting anew on the writings of Donna Haraway. While Hawking's perspective is the logical outcome of a vision of science that is instrumental, activist, and extropian, Haraway's approach is the opposite. Her scientific vision comprises "commingling" and "co-constituting" because her thought is a sustained, critical response to a four-hundred-year scientific history of use and abandon involving successively animals, plants, (human) bodies, and perhaps now the universe itself. For Haraway, science as we know it has always involved an extranatural, extracorporeal flight from our bodies, species, planet, from our "inappropriate/d" selves. Seeking a disjunctive break with the dominant spirit of technological transcendentalism, Haraway turns in another direction, away from virtual fantasies of the human species in a (space) bubble toward an immensely patient, meticulously detailed description of the geography of (scientific) pain out of which we have emerged and on behalf of which we have been fated to know ourselves in opposition to those companion species—gender, sexuality, race, and class—that commingle with and constitute our very own bodies.

To speak of Haraway as a major contributor to feminist discourse is also to recognize that in the thought of this inappropriate/d thinker, in the twists and knots and shifting stories of the dominations and powers of the women's bodies of which she writes, there is always the spark of something larger, something more encompassing of the paradoxes of the human condition itself. For that is what we are discussing—not a traditional feminist theorist who would seek to essentialize away gender differences in a language of absolute identity nor a thinker who would recover the always unsituated language of the repressed, the unspoken, the unspeakable from the multiplicity that is a woman's experience in the world, only to alienate it in the Archimedean tongue of constructivism, but a feminist struggling to ally the fate of gender and sexuality, the fate of women, with the commingled, co-constituted fate of animals and plants and cyborgs and aliens, and, yes, with the full spectrum of the gendered and the transgendered, the transsexual and the transvestite. Always a (feminist) theorist in and of hybridity in opposition to the "universal sameness" of the father's (scientific) word, Haraway makes of her thought a heuristic of the hybrid— hybrid concepts, words, punishments, pleasures, and, indeed, hybrid bodies of the cybernetic organisms of animals and vegetation and air and flesh, which promise to be our real companion species in the digital future. Conceived as the site of "multiple intersections" of power as opposed to an "unmarked universal," the hybrid body has its own eventual outcome rendered uncertain from the first moment of its theoretical conception. Will hybrid bodies of the future represent the psychopathology of scientific–technical objects in the making, or will the concept of hybridity itself constitute a way of living at the creative borderlands of all the broken (universal) identities of the future?

Listening to Simians

> If something is to stay in memory, it must be burned in: only that which never ceases to hurt stays in the memory—this is the main cause of the oldest (unhappily also the most enduring) psychology on earth.
> —Frederich Nietzsche, *On the Genealogy of Morals*

Written almost a century apart, Nietzsche's *On the Genealogy of Morals* has finally found its perfect doppelganger in Haraway's *Primate Visions,* but not as twin elements of a shared political vision: Nietzsche's reflections on ressentiment as the highest value of modernity can be so acute precisely because he is in his own persona the embodiment of "completed nihilism," and Haraway can so powerfully articulate multiple sites of inappropriate/d subjects because her thought eloquently represents the "insurrection of knowledge" alluded to by Foucault. Here the unmarked universal that is Nietzsche stands at one remove from the marked tracings that are the essence of Haraway's political critique. But for all these ostensible differences, a direct pathway opens between these texts: one an impassioned diagnosis of the melancholic ruins of late-nineteenth-century modern history focused on ressentiment as the highest value of Western rationality, the other a searing genealogy of the logic of scientific ressentiment in the twilight moments of late-twentieth-century experience. *Primate Visions* is in effect the theoretical equivalent of an experimental verification, all the more persuasive because it was never intended to be so, of what might now be thought of as *On the Genealogy of (Scientific) Morals*.

Not that this is Haraway's intention. Focused on the interrelated histories of paleoanthropology, biology, and media representations across the span of the twentieth century, this text announces itself as a critical exploration of "gender, race, and nature in the world of modern science." As such, its aims are (anthropologically) specific, namely, to focus on the research literature, field experiments, media representations, and art installations by which the scientific apparatus has colonized simians to demonstrate how gender, race, and nature are themselves deeply inflected sites of power, class, and patriarchy—the social detritus of an approach to nature, to the study of monkeys and apes—in which the domination of (reified) nature will come to mirror the domination of (reified) humanity.

With this project in mind, Haraway is theoretically relentless. Overcoming traditional boundaries among knowledge, power, and (capital) accumulation, Haraway relates the twentieth-century story of the scientific conquest of Africa again and again in terms that entangle paleoanthropology and multinational corporations, decolonization and "multinational primatology," "monkeys and monopoly capitalism," all culminating in a radically revised version of primate studies as a "genre of feminist theory." In this text, present and future finally yield to critical scholarship on the shared anthropological *past* from which we have emerged and through which we have come to negotiate a sex, a gender, an identity, a species. Displaced from their customary origins in the logic of empire, methods of scientific investigation are transformed into a forensics of primatology. Like an astral projection, the history of African primates is reinscribed as part of a larger technical project, becoming "a pilot plant for human engineering," a "taxidermy of the Garden of Eden," a "semiotics of the naturalistic field," a "technology of love," a "bio-politics of a multicultural field," a "Teddy Bear Patriarchy." It is as if for one instant the closed self-referential framework of the modern scientific epistēmē is shattered by the power of insistent, critical questions, finally breaking apart under this pressure into its constituent elements of race, class, and gender. Read as a political economy of paleoanthropology, *Primate Visions* discloses a history of scientific cruelty associated with the (research) harvesting of monkeys and apes by multinational corporations interested in eugenic experiments. Interpreted under the (Foucauldian) sign of power–knowledge, this is a material analysis of the circulatory flows of race, gender, sexuality, and class in which simians are inscribed as premonitory signs of our own colonization. Approached as an important dimension of the "politics of being female," Haraway can assert that "Women's Place is in the Jungle" because in the harsh history associated with the patriarchal law of "universal sameness"—in this anthropological fiction made fact of gendered man as the "unmarked signifier"—there is to be found the innermost generative codes of an increasingly violent sexual (human) economy. A *socialist* on the question of capital accumulation, a *feminist* on the question of patriarchy, a *deep ecologist* on the question of primates, an *antiracist* on the question of the topologies of colonial domination, and a *rebel* on behalf of subjugated knowledge on the question of officially authorized science, Haraway transforms *Primate Visions* from a critical study of primatology in the modern era, with its alliance between scientific knowledge and power and capital, into something else—an insurrection of the multiple, the interrupted, the hybrid. A creative opening to the future, *Primate Visions* listens carefully to our companion species—monkeys and apes—for what they have to tell us about the complicated histories of women, science, and capitalism.

The practice of listening to simians is immediately rewarding. Noting ominously that "sadism is a shadow twin to humanism," *Primate Visions* comprises an essential primer on what Western culture—its reason, bodies, gaze, desires, subjectivity, nature, race, gender—has first done to itself to practice sadism toward simians with a good (scientific) conscience. Read in reverse image—this time not so much a study of twentieth-century primatology as an extended, late-twentieth-century meditation on scientific nihilism—*Primate Visions* represents, in effect, a chilling account of sadism from the perspective of monkeys and apes. Genealogically, everything is vicariously, and viciously, present in the mirror of (African) nature. The color of "whiteness" is inscribed as part of the master chromatics of Western colonization; race is subsumed in the dialectic of master–slave; the masculine is constructed as the "unmarked gender"; white women are reduced to "mediators" between nature and culture; monkeys and apes are visualized as subjects of visualization; and everywhere there is a strategy of alienation so extreme, so intense (from research institutes and multinational corporations to the media documentaries of National Geographic), that the (Western) world has come to be haunted by its primatology.

How could it be otherwise? Long before the anthropological study of monkeys and apes, before even the projection of the dreams of biology onto primatology, the cold winds of predatory nihilism blew through the body of humanism. Scientific in its justification, technological in its instrumentalities, coded by the crusading spirit of good conscience, objectified in the languages of racism and colonialism, this expression of nihilism assumed the life-form of biopolitics. Here race would be invented as a "natural–technical object," signifying power through its "location in nature." Consider, for example, Haraway's typologies of the purely *virtual* experience that is whiteness and blackness:

> Black people were the *beast*; it is written into the history of lynching and into the history of biology. It is their accepting touch, coded back onto animals, that was so ardently sought in the ongoing western narratives of threatened apocalypse.[2]
>
> In a broad range of popular and official discourses in the west, perhaps especially in the former white settler colonies like the U.S., *white* is a color code for bodies ascribed the attributes of

mind, and thus symbolic power, not to mention other forms of power, in social practices, like "intelligence" tests. The *body* is coded darker, denser, less warm and light, less constituted by number. . . . Without its own principle of order, the body is properly the subject of control and the object of appropriation.[3]

Anticipating the analysis of Paul Gilroy's *Against Race,* with its critical theorization of the purely artificial character of race itself, there are deep affiliations here with the political logic of Franz Fanon, who, in his 1959 speech to the Congress of Black African Writers and Artists, had the following to say about the biological, the racial, component of the anticolonial struggle:

Three years ago at our first congress I showed that, in the colonial situation, dynamism is replaced fairly quickly by a substantification of the attitudes of the colonising power. The area of culture is then marked off by fences and signposts. These are in fact so many defense mechanisms of the most elementary type, comparable for more than one good reason to the simple instinct for preservation. The interest of this period for us is that the oppressor does not manage to convince himself of the objective non-existence of the oppressed nation and its culture. Every effort is made to bring the colonised person to admit the inferiority of his culture which has been transformed into instinctive patterns of behaviour, to recognise the unreality of his "nation," and, in the last extreme, the confused and imperfect character of his own biological structure.[4]

If Haraway's thought can parallel the thought of Fanon and Gilroy concerning the *political* construction of race, it is perhaps because, as a practicing biologist, she has actually deconstructed the life sciences from the inside. Exploring from a privileged, interior viewpoint the complicity of the life sciences in the histories of colonialism and racism, Haraway develops a devastating portrait of the artifactuals produced by Western humanism. Not an extrinsic critique somehow distanced from the dynamism of the scientific gaze, Haraway's thought is fully revelatory of the complex folded logic of science, with its oppositional struggles of sameness and difference—but not only this. What lends her thought its particular fascination is its ability to simultaneously weave together the story of vivisectionist (scientific) knowledge and the rhythms of a greater epic, namely, the narrative lines of science itself, as part of a larger historical project—Western expansionist narratives associated with racism and colonialism as symptomatic of the historical project of completed nihilism.

Specifically, while the various chapters of *Primate Visions* represent detailed case studies of the twentieth-century life sciences in relationship to the history of simians, there is in this writing an elusive hint of the unrepresentable, of that which does not wish to be named directly, hovering at the invisible margins of the text, barely detectable, its presence, though, almost tangible as the dynamism of the greater historical project pushing forward the narrative lines on which the artifactual world of racism and colonialism has been built. While Haraway privileges the act of storytelling as an essential aspect of a feminist methodology—a way of seeing that challenges the hermetic world of (patriarchal) representations with the specificities of "situated knowledge"—there is also the possibility that Haraway is herself caught up in a story definitely not of her own making but of which she is a brilliant point of illumination. On the surface, hers is a story of the representational logic of modern power. About this, Haraway is explicit:

> Once again, the old western dream of perfect representation surfaces [with] reality as an imperturbable asymptote, not itself deeply constituted by their own multiple practices.[5]

But for all of that, her thought can illuminate the scientific–technical project of knowledge because it names the unnamable, transforming the study of life sciences from an exclusively epistemological project to a critical meditation on something more ontologically primary—the study of science itself as the highest exemplar possible of what Nietzsche warned would be the one limit science itself would never transgress: the *will to truth.* This is precisely why Haraway is Nietzsche's *overcoming,* that epochal moment when the scientific consciousness of a practicing biologist becomes fully, and critically, self-conscious of science itself as a will to truth, with all that implies for questions of knowledge, power, and cruelty. How else to explain the profound supplementaries of *Primate Visions,* its insistence that the scientific–technical project exceeds its received epistemological jurisdiction, becoming a sustained exercise in "sadism"?

The deconstruction is total. Nothing is spared. Sweeping aside illusions concerning the so-called autonomy of the liberal subject, Haraway states that "sadism produces the self as fetish, an endlessly repetitive project."[6] Refusing to disconnect knowledge from the ritualistic practices of power, Haraway sums up the dialectic of enlightenment in this way:

> Sadism is about the structure of scientific vision, in which the body becomes a rhetoric, a persuasive language linked to social practice. The final cause, or telos, of that practice is the production of the unmarked abstract universal, man.[7]

With this, Haraway's thought rises beyond itself, representing in all its clinical brutality the *self-overcoming* of science. The will to truth is everywhere in *Primate Visions.* To its construction of nature as a laboratory of observation, experimentation, and demonstration, the will to truth produces a chilling register of body-effects: the *masculine* is the "unmarked gender";[8] the *female* is "his product, his reflection, perfectly mirroring his fantasy";[9] *women and animals* are set on "as body with depressing regularity in the working of the mind/body binarism in story fields, including scientific ones";[10] and *colored women* are "so closely held by the category animal that they can barely function as mediators in texts produced within white culture."[11]

> In those cultural fields, colored women densely code sex, animal, dark, dangerous, fecund, pathological. The "body" in revolt is often accused of irrational "terrorism." In the United States, political imaginations of white people color terrorists as dark, and dark people as dangerous. The body in western political theory is not capable of citizenship (rational speech and action); the body is merely particular, not general, not mindful, not light. It is sex (women) to mind (man); dark (colored) to light (white). The body is nature to mind of culture; in primate narratives, white women negotiate the chasm.[12]

Decades after these words were written, the specter of the "irrational terrorism" of the "body in revolt" outruns its origins in the colonial imagination to become the psychogeography of the contemporary war on terrorism, except now it is no longer only colored women who are coded "animal, dark, dangerous, fecund, pathological" but also people of religion—Muslims, specifically— who are retranslated into increasingly violent fantasies concerning the always threatening outsider, maintained in a constant state of suspicion as potential terrorists. And not only Muslims, but the "body in revolt" is now marked as a subject of "irrational terrorism": *sexually,* the officially undifferentiated bodies of gays, lesbians, transgenders, transsexuals; *politically,* the bodies of dissidents, antiwar activists, the antiglobalization movement; and *culturally,* the bodies of performance artists, poets, writers, actors. Everywhere the specter of (statist) power with its awesome capacity to define normative regimes of inclusion and exclusion, to nominate scapegoats, to articulate the terms of sacrificial violence extends its circulatory flows deeply into the complex subjectivity of bodies in revolt. Today the body in revolt is animal to the mind of power, darkness to the light of surveillance, marked in relationship to the unmarked sign of state terrorism. That state surveillance now seeks to detect the *preconscious intentions* of its domestic political subjects, that power obsessively occupies itself with deep mining the data archive (telephone, banking, travel, credit card records), only confirms the accuracy of the proposition that what power fears most, what power can only speak of as irrational terrorism, is the body in revolt.

Consequently, in Haraway's analysis, we are present at the very inception and now actualized future of the body in revolt—liberal subjectivity. Here the narrative of the liberal subject is brought to the surface of critical consciousness, with all its bodily productions, nature constructions, binary gender divisions, sexual traumas, and racist typologies. This is a liberal subjectivity literally formed simultaneously as subject and object of a narrative structure in which the qualities of the cosmos itself—light and darkness—are transcribed into a political catechism of power and terrorism. Produced by a will to truth burning the tutelary regimes associated with the liberal body—the truth of its sex, its gender, its color, its affiliations, its imaginations, its enemies—into its subjectivity, its flesh, its actions as a mnemonics of pain, liberal subjectivity has always been hybrid, artifactual, part simulacrum and part flesh. Never having had an originary presence in the world, always fantasizing itself as a product of "self-birthing"—a bodily production in and on behalf of narratives of power, racism, and colonialism—the liberal subject comes into the world as the psychopathology necessary to realize the historical project of complete nihilism.

There is a longer chain of *being bodily* present in this writing. Certainly it is a critical reflection on the production of liberal subjectivity, but there is also, perhaps hidden from immediate view, the Christian body which precedes this and on account of which *Primate Visions* represents a fundamental encounter with the ruling psychopathologies of Western cultural history itself. If the scientific narrative could be so obsessed with the body as "properly the subject of control and object of appropriation," perhaps it is because science is itself a latecomer to more extended historical narratives concerning the body. Perhaps *ontological preconditioning* that would later become the scientific construction of nature and human nature was already set in place by the much earlier body of Christian confessionality. If the unmarked (masculinist) gender could be produced as a hygienic dialectic of "self-birthing" and "sadism," maybe this is derivative from the earlier Christian insurrection against embodied knowledge. When the confessional body is marked by the binaries of grace (light) and sin (darkness), when the confessional body is produced with a debt to pay (original sin), then it is only a short psychological step from the death of the (Christian) god to the death of the (scientific) human.

Like a complex mandala, the story of the narrative structures associated with scientific vision opens up onto an inner Christian vista—the "primate vision" of evil and good, sin and grace. More than either a critical epistemology or insightful ontology, Haraway's real focus is eschatological—the study of the contemporary historical epoch as end times. Perhaps *Primate Visions* is an effective history of scientific vision as a secondary sign of the evacuated body of Christian confessionality, exposing everything in its historical trajectory to the more primitive movements of ressentiment, bad conscience, guilt over original indebtedness, ascetic priests cracking the chestnuts of petty grievances—disappearing animals; annihilating nature; altering the direction of ressentiment; coding the body by its sexuality, gender, and race; and transforming liberal subjectivity into an empty looking-machine.

About this, she is decisive in her historical judgments. Not only is "sadism the structure of scientific visions"[13] but sadism is not held to lie "at least originally, in the fact of causing repeated pain to animals in the course of experiments":[14]

> Rather, the sadism is the organizer of the narrative plot and part of the material apparatus for the cultural production of meanings; sadism is about meanings produced by particular

structures of vision, not about pain. In fact, sadism is about pleasure in vision; it is an erotic visual discipline for self-objectification.[15]

If the liberal subject is the psychopathology necessary for the circulation of the will to truth, its manifestations will not be confined to the language of pain but to the pleasure of an "erotic visual discipline for self-objectification." Important ethical consequences follow from this statement. When sadism is "the organizer of the narrative plot," when sadism is the animating energy for the creation of the "material apparatus for the cultural production of meanings," when sadism can be said to be about vision, not pain, then our very identity is rendered deeply equivocal. If we would not passively consent to regimes of sadism, then everything must be called into question, deconstructed, fully exposed—certainly the outer ring of sadism, the narrative codes of race, gender, and sex, but with much more difficulty, the inner rings of sadism, the circulation of sadism in the form of "meanings," in structures of "vision." When sadism can be viewed as deeply erotic, deeply felt as part of the visual discipline of self-objectification, at that point we know that the end times of *Primate Visions* is truly our deepest selves, our identities, our bodies:

> How to look is built into the spectacle, as aggression and anxiety are transmuted into the gold of the perfect image; the simulation or the copy that exceeds the original, whose independent existence may in any case, in the narrative, be doubted. Visual inspection, always the privileged form of knowing for western scientists, shows only the reflection, copy, substitute, fetish, in an endless chain of image-signifiers.[16]

However, *if* sadism cannot be held at a distant remove from our "look" as the look necessary for the production of the spectacle itself, *if* it is *our* identity that is the (willing) agent of "visual inspection," *if* the image-repertoire is (technically) indigenous to the who we are and what we would like to become, is it really possible to overcome sadism without overcoming liberal subjectivity itself? And would this self-overcoming of (scientific) sadism represent a fundamental rupture with the language of nihilism or only its most profound perpetuation? That is, would the self-overcoming of sadism by the "situated knowledge" of hybrid bodies constitute a definite conclusion to the (scientific) history of self-objectification or, in the curious way of all metaphysics, the pathway—all the more important for its unexpectedness—by which the meaning of *being body, being nature, being hybrid* opens up to us in the twenty-first century? In expressing her preference to be a cyborg rather than a goddess, is Haraway's ultimate fate to be the goddess of paradox?

Listening to Cyborgs

Such chilling visions of the sadism of (scientific) reason can emanate from Haraway's theory because all her thought is inspired by a powerful critical countermovement. One of the few contemporary theorists whose thought is epistemologically double-tracked—tracing both the logic of the scientific epistēmē and that which it excludes, silences, and crashes—Haraway's lasting contribution may be to rekindle an alternative vision of science, a *transformative science,* which, while fully intimate with the deepest codes of science and technology, undermines the perfect representational spectacle of (masculinist) science by a new feminist ethics. Avoiding both cybernetic determinism and feminist essentialism, Haraway encourages the production of a deeply feminist vision of hybrid bodies, inflected by paradox, motivated by "situated knowledge," self-conscious of the assemblages of power involved in the construction of race, gender, class, and sexuality, and living at the borderlands of a new form of critical politics that resists the absolute, refuses the identitarian, reveling in the imperfect, the impure, the rupture, the difference.

More than is customary, Haraway's feminism contributes to a fundamentally new way of understanding nature and, by implication, the damaged human nature that is liberal subjectivity. Here feminist theory finally becomes a mode of being *in and for itself,* emerging directly from the "situated knowledge" of the hybrid bodies so characteristic of cybernetic societies while, at the same moment, rethinking those hybrids of cyborgs, women, animals, and plants under the sign of social justice. That Haraway actually envisions a radically different way of *being scientific–technical,* an alternative approach to nature seeking to recapture unrealized, perhaps lost, connections, may be due to the fact that she herself is always already hybrid—part feminist, part cyborg, part companion species. Indeed, there is in all of Haraway's work a subtle but powerful sign of a nomadic thinker whose intellectual migration often assumes the form of a homecoming—a curve of (theoretical) light that accelerates a great distance into the galaxy of science only to bend at a decisive moment, tracing a path to the lost horizon of a feminism that would (finally) be spoken, of a woman's way of being in the world that would finally be situated, of stories about companion races, warring classes, intelligent cyborgs, and complicated genders that would finally be recognized for their dynamic complementarities.

And just in time. In contemporary politics, we are desperately in need of an alternative way of approaching nature—a radically different way of understanding the complex mediations of nature(s) that is the world today. If Haraway's writings can privilege mediations and materialities and (historical) specificities, then any critical reflection on this goddess of paradox should seek to honor the name of Haraway by situating her knowledge in the real material circumstances of the world-situation in which she writes. Deliberately never unsituated, her writings run parallel to the great cultural debates of our times, sometimes as feminist insurgency, at other points as a transformative science, and always as a still unappreciated source of wisdom offering a way through the global environmental crisis that futures the world.

Quite specifically, too. For example, *Simians, Cyborgs, and Women* challenges received narratives of instrumental science by theorizing a beautifully prodigal vision of science under the feminist sign of an inappropriate/ed other. Focusing on the specter of genetic determinism, *Modest Witness* offers a sustained ethical critique of the apparatus of power associated with biopolitics as well as another way of thinking at the borderlands of our shared genetic heritage. A very personal self-overcoming of "The Cyborg Manifesto," *The Companion Species Manifesto* creatively, and passionately, turns away from an exclusively technological vision of being to negotiate something more deeply complicated, namely, the how and why of human–animal communication. With its "situated knowledge" of human encounters with cyborgs, genes, and dogs, Haraway's thought is actually a form of time travel, meditating on the future consequences of different constructions of nature amid the present wreckage of (our) centuries-long experiment in technological eugenics.

The environmental urgency of such analysis is very apparent. For example, William Leiss, one of the world's leading thinkers in the area of technology and risk *(The Domination of Nature, Risk and Responsibility, Under Technology's Thumb),* recently posed this question about the future of biogenetics:

> Where does this path lead? The science of genomics intends to characterize fully the complete DNA for all living things, plants and animals (including ourselves) alike—or, at least, all of them which hold any interest for us. It also intends to understand completely the mechanisms whereby genes do their work—how they create the proteins that then produce the first cells, then tissues, and then complete organs, including the brain, how they are switched on and off, how and why "mistakes" may occur (giving birth to inherited diseases, including serious psychological disorders) and how their "outputs" might be modified or enhanced. Genomics will wish to complete its

knowledge of how a gene might be entirely deleted from a DNA sequence, or added to it where it has never before existed, and what the consequences are of doing so (we already know there are many unintended secondary effects from adding or deleting particular genes).

There is a great prize lurking in the background—namely, to know how to manipulate the genes that code for the development of the most complex structure in all of nature, namely the human brain. Recently, the Paul Allen Foundation, based in Seattle, announced a plan to fund neurogenetic research designed to identify—within a period of five years—all the genes responsible for the brain's structure and properties. And when that is done, as it surely will be, the scientists will turn to us and ask: What would you like us to do with this knowledge?[17]

And not just the brain, but why not "genes on a chip"? A recent announcement out of San Francisco has said,

The lofty goal of personalized medicine came one step closer to reality when two companies—rivals Affymetrix and Agilent Technologies—produced so-called "gene chips,"—dime-sized pieces of glass infused with genetic material. Employing semiconductor manufacturing technology, workers "print" genes one molecule at a time onto the glass until they stand up like microscopic skyscrapers, each about 25 molecules tall. Researchers then drop onto the chips specially tagged RNA, which serves as the messenger between DNA blueprints and a cell's protein-making machinery. The portion of a chip on which genes interact with the RNA will be fluorescent, highlighting bad genes that may need a closer look.

Some researchers envision a day when pediatricians and other physicians will be armed with these chips, technically called microarrays. The hope is that a drop of a newborn's blood can quickly be converted into a genome on a chip. From there, the doctor can determine the baby's predilection to disease and other genetic traits. "This is starting to get really cool and it's sending shivers up my spine in a good and bad way," said Dietrich Stephan of the nonprofit Translational Genomics Research Institute in Scottsdale, Arizona.[18]

The report concludes that "it will take some time for scientists to figure out how to interpret all the data that the gene chips equipped with the complete genome can spit out." Once Moore's law, which predicted the exponential growth of memory in computing and semiconductors, is applied to the human genome, then genes on a chip indicate that the natural body is in for a fast speedup, for an accelerating rate of genetic intervention intent on redesigning the body and its codes. There are hints here: not just genes on a chip but something more specific—brains on a chip, emotions on a chip, personalities on a chip, maybe even you and me on a chip.

The actual situation today may be that we are living in a culture of twenty-third-century engineering and nineteenth-century ethics. Consequently, to develop an ethics equal to the power of genetic determinism, it is crucial to consider which vision of science—instrumental or transformative science—should guide the future of biogenetics, a scientific vision that allies itself dynamically with the language of the genome or a transformative science that both explores creative possibilities associated with biogenetics and problematizes the ideology of genetic determinism in terms of its genealogy and purposes. This ethical choice is crucial since the compelling rhetoric of genetic determinism is on the verge of quickly overwhelming traditional forms of ethical debate. Without any real public discussion, we are already living in a technoculture that has implicitly committed itself to genetically reengineering the body to facilitate health and longevity. One moment, we are living in a digital society with its wired future, and in the next instant, the codes of digitality have themselves been superseded by the more powerful drive to the fully realized genome—a world that is authentically posthuman not only because, for the first time, the (human) body has itself been made the active subject of genetic redesign but also because the will to genomics has effectively declared an end to the concept of the human species, substituting the potentially perilous notion that species-life itself is a proper object for a freely inventive genetic makeover. In essence, posthumans would be the first beings to consciously prototype their own species extinction, making of this mass extinction a dizzying whirlwind of (cybernetic) publicity: genes on a chip, augmented intelligence, hardwiring the human nervous system to the cellular automata of the media; and genetically mining, transcribing, and pirating the human genetic heritage. Definitely post-McLuhan, posthumans are also post-Darwin. As genetic pilgrims traveling in the twenty-first century, we are living at that epochal transitional moment when the body itself is being swiftly brought under the control of a probing, creative, radically experimental bioscience, mapped for its genetic secrets, redesigned by recombinant genetics that clip strands of DNA—hybridized, sampled, and sequenced. Today McLuhan's celebrated image of the global village has been replaced by the deterministic drive toward the global genome.

In the midst of this powerful will to genomics, Haraway proposes a critical, comprehensive, and eloquent vision of transformative science. Refusing to consider ethics outside the lived materiality of bioscience, Haraway reinvents a model of ethics that is itself directly emergent from the (genomic) times in which we live. To the emphasis of instrumental science on the representational powers of visualization, Haraway proposes that we consider anew the importance of scientific vision. To the binary world of normal science, with its strict lines of division between objective reality and subjective perception, Haraway privileges the search for intermediations and interconnections. To the extropian belief that the human species will be effectively bypassed by its technological progeny, Haraway is persuasive in arguing that we are all cyborgs now, interpolated assemblages of technology, flesh, and desire as a result of our common, companion species heritage. To the calculative drive toward the genomic harvesting of our shared bioheritage, Haraway works to create a transformative science that creates dynamic complementarities between technologies of creation and nurturing. To the "informatics of domination" of instrumental science, she responds with a creative vision stressing the contingent, the partial, the interruption.

It is definitely not customary for feminist theory to be so attentive to the presence among us humans of cyborgs, replicants, zombies, and aliens. It is even less usual for feminist theory to take its performative cues from the language of hard science itself. Yet this is precisely the charismatic quality of Haraway's feminism—not for her a feminism that would recapitulate the identity-logic of traditional patriarchy nor a mode of feminism that would disappear the contingency of life itself (the partiality, indeterminacy, and necessary ambiguities of flesh and desire) into either the larger cybernetic drives of codework or the more vitalistic currents of genetic determinism. Refusing the extremes of (gendered) overidentification and (genetic) undersignification, Haraway does that which is most unusual, and for that very reason, most ethically creative—she listens to the cyborgs.

That her hearing privileges the question of the cyborg is evident everywhere in her writings. It explains the brilliant prescience of "The Cyborg Manifesto"; the interpretive acuteness of her analysis of "the biopolitics of postmodern bodies" in terms of immune system discourse; the privileging of "partial perspective" as a way of revealing the "situated knowledges" of feminism in science; and her deeply insightful observations on sociobiology and human engineering in the contemporary epoch. Breaking beyond the discursive limits of received theoretical analysis, Haraway actually sees—she brings into presence—the partial, the interrupted, the spliced, the remixed that populate the future of biopolitics.

And how could she not do this? As a feminist who writes very much in the tradition of women writers everywhere who have been forced, as a desperate matter of affirming the integrity of their own existence, to draw into reality those other sexes, other genders, other bodies, other desires that have been reduced to invisibility by the combined languages of power, science, and economy, Haraway must either listen to the partial stories of cyborgs, to the local histories of "companion species," to "modest witness" the (bioscientific) times in which she lives, or perish as a (feminist) thinker. That she can witness so well the advent of all the spliced bodies of the futures—cyborgs, aliens, replicants, and zombies—that she can listen so intently to the partial, connected, complicated histories of the bodies toward which we are quickly evolving; that she can intuit otherwise invisible connections among divided species is due to the fact that Haraway's "listening" is always done best with her eyes. Well ahead of the bodily recombinants of the genetic future, Haraway has already developed an imaginative form of intellectual reasoning that splices together the previously divided organs of looking and hearing into a search for a new method of "scientific vision." Not waiting passively for the capricious experiments of biotechnology to produce spliced bodies, Haraway has made of her own mind a biopolitics on creative hyperdrive. Deeply immersed in the (bio)scientific disciplines, always distancing herself from the seductions of technological representationality by feminist difference, continuously provoking boundary breakdowns in her own thought by refusing to assent to an anthropomorphic species-hierarchy, Haraway is a theorist of the splice. Long before bioscience can ideologically overdetermine the world, Haraway has made of her own thinking a model of a creative biogenetics—spliced, hybridized, interfacing, transcribing, always partial, always disturbing the boundary and remixing the difference. Against the coming sovereignty of the overvisualized, overexposed bodies of the culture of the copy, Haraway can so persuasively introduce the counterchallenge of new scientific "revisionings" because she is, above all, a transgenic feminist.

Transgenic Feminism

> The perfection of the full defended, "victorious" self is a chilling fantasy, linking phagocytotic amoeba and moon-voyaging man cannibalizing the earth in an evolutionary teleology of post-apocalypse extra-terrestrialism. It is a chilling fantasy, whether located in the abstract space of national discourse, or in the equally abstract spaces of our interior bodies.[19]

A shape-shifter in the world of technology, transgenic feminism lives in the unsettled boundaries between the organic and the artificial, the genomic and the embodied. Fully attentive to the hard (inscriptive) lessons of genetic determinism, studying intently both oppressive and emancipatory strategies of bodily production, thinking of the world as an active agent and the body as a "material-semiotic" actor, transgenic feminism understands technology itself as a "coding trickster with whom we must learn to converse."[20]

In the absence of this conversation, there is only the darkness of gathering storm clouds on the political horizon. Like a mirror of identity closed to anything but its own representation, the dominant (technological) discourses of neoliberalism and neoconservatism seemingly work to confirm the ineluctability of the imperialism of the "coding trickster." Everywhere now, from war technologies to the predatory language of genomics, there is a tangible hint of a greater violence rising—a fused spirit of a sacrificial public morality coupled with the redemptive hopes of an increasingly faith-based politics. Confronted with the demagogic winds signaling the arrival of this gathering storm, many critical traditions of thought have been quickly pushed aside, reduced to silence by the power of the "coding trickster" or rendered irrelevant on account of the fact that their received terms of critical analysis no longer accurately describe the radically changed nature of the present historical era.

But for all that, the coding trickster is not omnipotent. Outside the dominant regimes of knowledge, certainly unreported by the media, there is a multiplicity of democratic struggles, multiple "partial views" and "halting voices" finding common ground in their resistance to a coding trickster animated only by "chilling fantasies" of the extraterrestrial and postapocalyptic. It is to this larger, deeper stream of democratic movement struggles that the transgenic feminism of Donna Haraway makes its finest contribution. As the creative *overcoming* of feminism itself, transgenic feminism is that moment when the radical upsurge that is feminist struggle transforms itself from its exclusive preoccupation with a woman's natural essence to the problematic of *crossing boundaries* that is the real world of the coding trickster. This is why Haraway can assert so eloquently that today bodies are born, not made; that nature is constructed, not given; and that gender is a positional moment in a deeper ideological struggle:

> This is because feminist embodiment resists fixation and is insatiably curious about the webs of differential positioning. There is no single feminist standpoint because our maps require too many dimensions for that metaphor to ground our visions. But the feminist standpoint theorist's goal of an epistemology and politics of engaged, accountable positioning remains incredibly potent. The goal is better accounts of the world, that is, "science."[21]

And mapping is exactly what transgenic feminism does in brilliant detail. In Haraway's work, there are maps everywhere: maps to navigate "The Cyborg Manifesto," maps to better explore the world of primate visions, maps that creatively reenvision the oncomouse under the sign of genetic determinism, maps for visualizing the bifurcated regimes surrounding the "apparatus of bodily production," maps of "daughter of the man-hunters," maps for discovering elusive pathways around "sex, mind and profit," mappings of "theories of production and reproduction," and even genealogical maps for deciphering the enigmatic phrase "In the Beginning was the Word."

But most compelling of all, there is Haraway's mapping of the legacy codes of the coded trickster—her cartography of immune system discourse in "The Biopolitics of Postmodern Bodies." Decades after its first publication, her analysis of the changing meaning of the immune system is increasingly important as part of the larger debate on boundary exchanges among bodies, technology, and nature in the twenty-first century. Beyond its specific scientific determination, immune system discourse is one of the basic metaphors of contemporary life, ranging from ecological discourse concerning the impact of global warming, the role of the AIDS virus in weakening bodily immunity, and the battleship images of Star Wars to the generalized panic fear encouraged by the state as part of its media strategies involved in the production of a compliant domestic population. Long in advance of a popular culture that now focuses its sense of anxious vulnerability on the breakdown of immunity systems—medical, cultural, military, climatic—Haraway noted that scientific discourses are "lumpy; they contain and enact condensed contestations for meanings and practices":[22]

> The chief object of my attention will be the potent and polymorphous object of belief, knowledge, and practice called the immune system. My thesis is that the immune system is an elaborate icon for principal systems of symbolic and material "difference" in late capitalism. Pre-eminently a twentieth-century object, the immune system is a map drawn to guide recognition and misrecognition of self and other in the dialectics of Western biopolitics.[23]

Late capitalist society is dependent on the production of a supposedly self-sufficient "self" coded by the illusion of immunity, with fixed borders between inner and outer worlds, capable of scaling up technologically in case of boundary invasions. Border breakdowns involving immunity system discourse are the privileged site at which the most bitter, polemical, and potent "condensed contestations for meaning and practices" occur in contemporary society. This point is (politically) decisive since, as Haraway has argued in detail, we are always living in the splice of violent border crashes. Boundary disturbances are multiple at all the key localities of technology, humans, and nature, with porous, fluid negotiations marking exchanges between machines and humans and nature and culture. Quite the opposite of the established iconography of immune system discourse, we may well be living, in effect, in a culture of no immunity.

For transgenic feminism, the undermining of immune system discourse is a creative opening, not a cause for panic fear. After all, in her essay "Situated Knowledges," Haraway reflected on "persistence of vision" as the privileged sensory system of feminism. Insisting on the "embodied nature of all vision," reminding us that "vision can be a good thing for avoiding binary oppositions," she sought to reclaim the *durational* quality of "persistence of vision" as the form that *objectivity* takes for a feminist discourse that would escape the gaze of representation, evoking in its place a "conquering gaze from nowhere."[24] Indeed, if her words can plead "for a feminist writing of the body that metaphorically emphasizes vision again,"[25] it is because she senses clearly the dangers of technologies of (scientific) visualization that have about them the "perversity" of second birthing and disembodiment:

> The visualization technologies are without apparent limit; the eye of any ordinary primate like us can be endlessly enhanced by sonography systems, magnetic resonance imaging, artificial intelligence–linked graphic manipulation systems, scanning electron microscopes, computer-aided tomography scanners. . . . Vision in this technological feast becomes unregulated gluttony; all perspective gives way to infinitely mobile vision. . . . Like the god-trick, this eye fucks the world to make techno-monsters. Zoe Sofoulis calls this the cannibal-eye of masculinist extra-terrestrial projects for second-birthing.[26]

The concept of the "persistence of vision" anticipates Virilio's later theorization of *The Vision Machine* but adds to it something dramatically different, something that could only originate with an embodied feminism—an acute sensitivity to visualization technologies as possessing mythological qualities of cannibalism and self-birthing—an "eye [that] fucks the world to make techno-monsters."

Immune system discourse is also deeply involved with the creation of techno-monsters. In its traditional representation, immunity has been visualized in terms of an omnipotent "master control system or hyper-armed defense department."[27] Alienated from its environment, its mind abstracted from its body, fully alert to the threat of body invaders from an always threatening outer world, its consciousness split from its (biological) organs, the immunized body is the quintessential sign of the techno-monster become flesh, with the predictable result that the localized, organic, and hierarchical body of the eighteenth- and nineteenth-century became

> a relatively unambiguous locus of identity, agency, labor and hierarchicalized function. Both scientific humanisms and biological determinisms could be authorized and contested in terms of the biological organism crafted in post-eighteenth century life sciences.[28]

Breaking with a feminist politics of the body that would mirror the body as a "relatively unambiguous locus of identity, agency, labor and hierachicalized function," and refusing, in turn, the migration of gay and lesbian politics at the end of the twentieth century to embrace the "marked bodies" of exclusion ("Negritude, feminine writing, various separatisms") that define sex and gender identity in biomedical discourse, Haraway proposes a radically different vision of the hybrid body, with equally radical implications for body politics.

When the body is reenvisioned in terms of "cyborgs for earthly survival," when Haraway speaks of the body as a "material-semiotic actor" living in a distributed field of knowledge—organic, technological, textual—she stakes the future of body politics on a profoundly new (scientific) conception of bodily immunity. With the body cyborg, there is no longer ontological priority among the organic, textual, and technological, nor is there any necessary lessening of the mythical. Conceptualized as a problem of design and not the (essential) locus of consciousness, cyborgs are "coded texts" whose immunity has everything to do with controlling the rate and flow of boundary exchanges; where heterogeneous fields of contestation involving race and gender are less about essences than about "power-charged differences"; and where the privileged pathology is "stress"—the suppression of the immune system by communication breakdown. But of course, breakdowns are also opportunities for enhanced understanding of processes essential for survival from the periphery to the very centre of human attention.[29]

Faithfully scientific in aligning the construction of the body with leading cybernetic theorizations (from information theory to Richard Dawkins' *The Extended Phenotype*), Haraway's cyborg always has about it an element of genuine perversity. No sooner has naturalization been abandoned than she immediately deconstructs the history of cyborgs into its constituent narratives. Not for her a *rationalist* paradigm of cybernetics which would function to reinstall a "master control narrative." Instead, her thought privileges a heterogeneous, contested, interdependent, fluid vision of the "cyborgs for earthly survival" that our bodies and our hominid *selves* have become. ("Structural couplings give a better approach to perception than doctrines of representation."[30]) In this embodied vision, "context is a fundamental matter, not as surrounding 'information,' but as co-structure or co-text," just as much as immunity itself is about "constraint and possibilities for engaging in a world of 'difference,' replete with non-self."[31]

Consequently, while Haraway can conclude that the body is a "controlled accident, not the highest fruit of earth history's labour,"[32] her rethinking of the body with its vulnerabilities as an opening on to life itself, her *feminist* retranslation of current (biomedical) understandings of immunity as focused on boundary exchanges, has the very real merit of providing a desperately required feminist ecology for these crisis times:

> Immunity can also be conceived in terms of shared specificities: of the semi-permeable self, able to engage with others (human and non-human, inner and outer), but also with finite consequences; of situated possibilities and impossibilities of individuation and identification; and of partial fusions and dangers. The problematic multiplicities of postmodern selves must be brought into other emerging Western and multi-cultural discourses on health, sickness, individuality, humanity, and death.[33]

A technological feminist whose retheorization of the body parallels the most important scientific discoveries of the "biotech century," Haraway strips the study of hybridity of its previous romantic affiliations, inaugurating instead a creative vision of the body as a dynamic force field. Coded by the narratives of power yet remaining heterogeneous, local, and embodied, the body hybrid surfaces anew in a world of "co-texts" and "coupled structures." A "problematic multiplicity," the body hybrid can only know other "nonselves" by opening itself to new forms of reciprocal communication with all the hominids, animals, machines, aliens, zombies, and replicants of the future. In essence, if the body hybrid is not to be a copy of a master code, it must engage with the difficult heuristics of companion species. If there is no necessary immunity, there must definitely be (species) community.

The Double Helix of Feminism

> There are no pre-constituted subjects and objects, and no single sources, unitary actors, or final ends. In Judith Butler's terms,

there are only "contingent foundations"; bodies that matter. A bestiary of agencies, kinds of relatings, and scores of time trump the imaginings of even the most baroque of cosmologists. For me, this is what companion species signifies.[34]

Haraway's intimation is correct. Her migration from the machinic assemblages of "The Cyborg Manifesto" to the "dogs, people, and significant otherness" who populate *The Companion Species Manifesto* is very much feminist theory. Similar to her theoretical predilection for mapping opposing binaries—representation versus simulation; universal philosophies versus ethnophilosophies; organism versus biotic component—"The Cyborg Manifesto" and *The Companion Species Manifesto* represent a thought-machine for unconcealing, and thus overcoming, the binaries in her own feminist theory. Supposedly opposite pathways of thought—one cybernetic, the other organic; one "cyborgs for earthly survival," the other listening intently to our companion species—these two manifestos represent the twisted strands in the double helix of Haraway's feminism. That they move in opposing directions across (cybernetic) space and (dogland) time, that one is about speculative "reenvisioning" and the "significant otherness," that there is a very real tension in the curvature of their arguments, only means that, taken together, they represent the most intensive expressions possible of completed feminism.

Deep theoretical continuities run between the manifestos. Hovering over both is the philosophical shadow of Alfred North Whitehead's process philosophy, with its description of the concrete as a "concrescence of prehensions."[35] Reality is in motion, with beings "reaching into each other, through their 'prehensions' or *graspings*."[36] Haraway can claim that "the world is a knot in motion" because, understood as process, there is no room for binary dualisms, preestablished categories, unchanging classifications, or imposed hierarchies. "Beings reach into one another, grasping" for connection, "coupled structures," "problematic multiplicities," for other beings, other species with whom we are finally "co-constituting." This is as true of the liminal zone between flesh and machines illuminated by "The Cyborg Manifesto" as it is of those tentative, emergent expressions of evocative communication between hominids and animals that is the subject matter of *The Companion Species Manifesto.*

Departing from the classic pattern of political manifestos that privilege messages on behalf of future exclusions and power priorities, Haraway's manifestos do precisely the opposite. They are actually the fulfillment in practice of Whitehead's process philosophy—manifestos as knots in motion, in which first encounters take place between different species-beings reaching out to each other, grasping for co-constitution, for a minimal level of reciprocal communication. In the liquid space of difference between these manifestos, dogs, other animals, and significant others do not stop with humans but actually follow a great migration to the world of cyborgs, to those assemblages of flesh and machines lighting up the future of technological society. What counts here is not the mapping of borderlines but those liminal zones where boundaries begin to slip, where skin becomes less a passive covering than an active material–semiotic agent, and where other gestures, other voices, are finally understood as the basic co-texts of an approaching future of companion species.

The media theorist Marshall McLuhan once noted that technologies of communication sometimes reveal possibilities for what traditional religions have long recognized as epiphanies in human communication—the long-held mythic dream of universal human communication. There is very much the spirit of an epiphany in Haraway's two manifestos: not so much a religious epiphany, with its foreshadowing of the presence of divinity, but a feminist epiphany—the revelation of "world as a knot in motion." If Haraway can theorize so well the bifurcated world of process philosophy, if she can think almost instinctively in terms of liminality—material–semiotic actors, co-texts, coupled structures, co-constituting beings grasping toward each other—it is also because her thought has been touched deeply by Roman Catholicism:

> My soul marked indelibly by Catholic formation, I hear in species the doctrine of the Real Presence under both species, bread and wine, the transubstantiated signs of the flesh. Species is about the corporeal join of the material and the semiotic in ways unacceptable to the secular Protestant sensibilities of the American academy and to most versions of the human sciences of semiotics.[37]

Indeed, if, as the Roman Catholic theologian Etienne Gilson once claimed, Roman Catholicism runs parallel to the great cultural discoveries of the modern era, it is because the deep epistemology of Roman Catholicism, with its doubled liminality—sign–flesh, grace–bodies, sign–corporeality—has always anticipated the crucial struggles over the resolution of the problem of identity and difference so central to modern culture. That Haraway brushed against Roman Catholic epistemology in her early life, that she has attained a form of cultural attunement sensitive to stories of contradiction, conflict, and difficult entanglements, probably means that this wonderful apostate has translated into feminist theory the trinitarian formulation that was the Roman Catholic resolution to the problem of the divided world of the sacred and the human—trinitarian, that is, because between the metaphor of "The Cyborg Manifesto" and the metonymy of *The Companion Species Manifesto,* there is the third term of the feminism of Donna Haraway, connective, co-constituting, a thinker of knots in motion and coupled structures:

> In "The Cyborg Manifesto," I tried to write a surrogacy agreement, a trope, a figure for living within and honoring the skills and practices of contemporary technoculture without losing touch with the permanent war apparatus of a non-optional,

post-nuclear world and its transcendent, very material lies. Cyborgs can be figures for living within contradictions, attentive to the naturecultures of mundane practices, opposed to the dire myths of self-birthing, embracing mortality as the condition for life, and alert to the emergent historical hybridities actually populating the world at all its contingent scales.

However, cyborg figurations hardly exhaust the tropic work required for ontological choreography in technoscience. I have come to see cyborgs as junior siblings in the much bigger, queer family of companion species, in which reproductive biotech-nopolitics are generally a surprise, sometimes a nice surprise.[38]

In the usual way of things, who but a goddess of paradox could connect the figurative dots between cyborgs and companion species, writing an "ontological choreography" in which "reproductive biotechnopolitics" is reenvisioned as a "figure for living," a "historical hybridity," a sibling in the sprawling, contradictory, mortal "queer family of companion species"? In this (feminist) writing, technoscience is finally turned from the inside, its possibilities for self-birthing and contingent renewal vigorously choreographed in a theoretical insurgency representing, in all its vulnerability and creative power, the self-overcoming of science itself in the twenty-first century.

EPILOGUE:
BODIES AND POWER

What is the future of the body in a society inscribed by the regime of computation, mobilized by increasingly phantasmagoric visions of the war on terror, and resistant to the perspective of companion species?

The writings of Butler, Hayles, and Haraway are at the epicenter of contemporary political debate. Not only have they explored in theoretical detail the framework of contemporary subjectivity, whether cast in the language of gender, computation, or genomic biology, but they have done so in a way that has produced key visions of contemporary society. What is most evident in the intellectual trajectories traced by these three theorists is that in each instance, there has been a decided shift in their respective pathways of thought. While each writer may have begun with a specific problematic—gender construction for Butler, the entwinement of cybernetics and feminism for Haraway, and the paradoxical status of order and chaos for Hayles—the thematics of all three have increasingly converged on critical analysis of different bodily inflections in contemporary society.

Breaking with her previous engagement with "bodies that matter" and "gender trouble," Butler has refocused her thought on the problem of grievability, or, more to the point, absence of grievability, in contemporary subjectivity. Here the dark politics of the global war on terror seems to have inspired on Butler's part an internal shift in her thinking, away from a preoccupation with the signifying regimes of heterosexual normativity to a deeper reflection on a society that wrestles anew with the challenge of Antigone, namely, the question of love and grief in a state of unjust laws. With *The Psychic Life of Power, Precarious Life,* and *Frames of War,* Butler has in effect written the companion volume to *Antigone's Claim.* It's the very same with Hayles. She might have begun with a systematic exposition on the genealogy of computation, but increasingly, her work has focused on the complex interpellation of software code as its passes through the dense force fields of literature, society, and the multiple bodies of "writing machines." Refusing to settle for a form of cybernetic thought that takes up the project of positivism by digitizing the humanities, Hayles does something very different. Her overall project is not to adapt the humanities to the digital imperative but, in the way of all critical intellectuality, to actually humanize the digital. Hayles is insistent in her claim that beyond speech, writing, and gesture, the new language of the twenty-first century will be the critical study of codes. Particularly when the regime of computation is combined with emergent developments in neuroscience, the language of codes no longer remains external to the human sensorium but is effectively on the verge of interpolating the human brain. Consequently, Hayles can be so insistent about drilling the critical study of code into the literary cortex because of a larger cultural anxiety on her part concerning the fate of the body when code literally comes alive in the form of the "intelligent life" promised by genetic engineering.

So, then, with Butler and Hayles, we have two very critical images of the public situation, with Butler's focus on grief and terror matched by Hayles' equally public concern with the lack of cultural awareness in the age of computation. While Butler's eloquent reflections on grief in the age of terror most certainly circle back to classical reflections on power, injustice, and the rites of kinship as addressed in the intense brilliance that is *Antigone's Claim,* Hayles' appeal for cultural awareness of the yet unknown implications of the software culture finds resonance in a longer tradition of civil humanism. For contemporary subjectivity, the politics of terror and the regime of computation are the living space and time of the real world of globalization. Definitely not separate, the war on terror, with its surveillance apparatus, laws authorizing indefinite detention and preemptive arrest, and data mining focused on the body of the citizenry, is enabled by the regime of computation. At the same moment, the penetration of the regime of computation into the skin of humanity, including its order of perception, affect, social networks, and most intimate activities, carries with it something of what Jean Baudrillard once described as the "terrorism of the code." Could it be that what is really disowned, excluded, and repressed by the regime of computation is the possibility of a more general human grief concerning that which has been lost with the radiating triumph of computation?

The doubled themes of grief and terror, computation and disembodiment, find, I believe, their effective mediation in the thought of Donna Haraway. Precisely because the psychoanalytic concerns of Butler and the scientific preoccupations of Hayles share very little on the surface with Haraway's focus on thinking questions of gender and power, species-logic, and technology, Haraway has all the more powerfully translated questions of grief and terror, computation and disembodiment, into a form of thought that is, in effect, a way of working through the contemporary human condition. Grief and terror pervade Haraway's writings, from her earliest reflections on the dispossessed role of women generally and immigrant women's labor specifically in the "informatics of domination" to her studies of primates, cyborgs, and women, where the question of terrorism is always pronounced, from biological terrorism directed against animals to violence directed against all those who are effectively disavowed, excluded, and disappeared by regimes of power. Equally, themes of computation and disembodiment—the specter of posthuman identity—are explored in all her writings, from her reflections on informatics directly to critical analysis of the doubled identity of the photographic gaze. With this difference, though, perhaps mindful of the necessarily therapeutic strategy of working through grief for that which has been lost with the triumph of the technological mastery of social and nonsocial nature, Haraway actually develops a therapeutic regime on both an individual and planetary scale. That is, I believe, the true radical nature of the idea of "companion species": an ontological, then political, challenge to the prevailing order of things. *Companion Species* is how "precarious life" might finally learn to grieve the loss of kinship, love, and solidarity in the hypersolitude of human compassion encouraged by the war on terror. Rethinking ourselves, our bodies, our devices, as companion species might also be a way of addressing the growing reality of computation and disembodiment. Other animals, other devices, other ethnicities, other races, other religions: could all these be conceived as companion species? That is the dramatic possibility posed in all its contingency, complexity, and hybridity by the thought of Judith Butler, Katherine Hayles, and Donna Haraway.

Thinking the Future of Body Drift

And what of the future of body drift?

In the way of all thought, honoring the critical feminism of Butler, Hayles, and Haraway has meant brushing their thought against past, present, and future. Particularly with regard to the still unfolding future, theirs is a form of critical feminism that always seeks to overcome itself—overcome, that is, not in the sense of abandonment but in the sense of thinking what remains to be thought by critical feminism. In this sense, privileging contingency, complexity, and hybridity discloses at once a very real tension between the authorized claims to the putative unity of the body and the very material, very embodied struggles to transgress the codes, to undermine patterns of gender and sexual intelligibility, to subvert the primacy of (human) species logic. Of course, what remains to be thought are the historical ends of body drift. What is the likely direction of the drift that has caught our multiple bodies in its strong current?

Power Intermediating Life and Death

For example, consider the relationship of bodies and power. An immediate casualty of the concept of body drift is Michel Foucault's justly famous claim in the first volume of *The History of Sexuality* that power no longer speaks in the language of consanguinity but operates now according to a different normative standard—*power over life*.[1] Confronted by Foucault's claims creating a necessary alliance between power and life, contemporary bodily history is decidedly more ambivalent. Certainly it is the case that in the biotech century, power over life is, indeed, the driving force, the purely technological concept that will surely code the production of future bodies. Delirious experiments involving the creation of transgenic beings—strange intermediations of plants and animals with the cyborg and the human—are under way in many advanced genomic research labs around the globe. Already there are euphoric estimates that the human species is on the verge of being technically augmented into something dramatically new—a transhuman species. Of course, to this order of body drift, there is only silence in the face of the question, are we ethically prepared for the full consequences of power over life?

The traditional alliance of power and consanguinity—the entanglement of death, blood, and torture—has most definitely returned as a dominant, chilling marker of contemporary politics. More than ever, bodily multiplicity drifts in unanticipated directions—the body sometimes a religious instrument of political sacrifice, at other times a torture chamber inhabiting the dark cells and ghost prisons of sovereign tyrannies, and, increasingly, bodies inscribed by the fundamentalist language of "intelligent design" in Western societies. At the political minimum, the future of body drift is about the contested space of power itself. In the future, will power over life and power over death really remain simply equivalent forces in the framing of contemporary body politics? Or is a new twist in the ontology of power already under way, specifically, the interpellation of death and life as cynical signs of a form of power that never, in the first instance, had any real interest in life or death but only in the preservation of life and the securing of death as constitutive conditions for maintaining intact the cycle of power itself?

Or perhaps something else explains why power has drifted away from the binaries of life and death. Under the sign of body drift, power is increasingly circuited through the informational nervous system of technoculture. Yet, at the same time as power intimately intersects the regime of computation—electronic surveillance, data tracking, augmented communication, social networking—power itself adopts a political vocabulary that is replete with irreconcilable bitterness, atavistic motivations, and revenge-seeking behavior. For example, consider the vengeful politics of the body—purified, disciplined, constrained—that issues from resurgent conservative movements. Here, for all the technological utopias envisioned for the enhanced, upgraded digital body, the language of political choice is resolutely revenge-seeking; based on a perceived history of slights and injury; directed in every instance against the bodies of the excluded, the disavowed, the illegible; motivated by barely suppressed violence; and demonstrating all the classic psychological signs of repressing that which is actually most desired. Today, the politics of the body hovers between extropian visions of the fully augmented body transcending earthly decay and deeply ancient appeals to traditional expressions of recidivism, infused predominantly by primal male rage, always valorizing itself in the language of bodily purification.

So, then, for all the power of the technological sublime in circuiting bodies through the informational nervous system of digital culture, the material bodies of contemporary history are the object of purification campaigns launched by faith-based politics seemingly everywhere, if not submitted increasingly, in the case of women's bodies, to the deployment of state-sanctioned rape as a weapon of war by fearful tyrannies. Always, there is rage: male rage against women, rage against any sign of sexual difference, rage against gender outlaws, rage flowing from a mass politics of ressentiment.

In this context, we desperately require a theory of power—contingent, complex, hybrid—that finally moves beyond the closed binaries of life and death. The inestimable contribution of critical feminism is to have theorized power beyond the antinomies of life and death, a form of power that is pulled into a gap of its own making. Here power is conceived as somehow drifting between atavism and rationality, between juridical regimes aimed at the protection of life and extrajuridical uses of violence against those who would speak the language of freedom to power. When public life on a global scale represents a dense twisting back and forth of the rational and irrational, the technocratic and the sacrificial, reason and faith, then the understanding of contingent power provided by critical feminism is an emblematic guide to the future of body drift. The thought of Butler, Hayles, and Haraway may have begun within a specific feminist register, but the consequences of the collision of their thought with the demands of the day has resulted in their being thinkers at the height of their times, nowhere more so than in their understanding of bodies and power.

Consequently, will the future of body drift give rise to what the philosopher, George Grant, has described as the "plush patina of hectic subjectivity lived out in the iron maiden of an objectified world inhabited by increasingly objectifiable beings"?[2] Or does body drift as rehearsed so eloquently in the thought of Butler, Hayles, and Haraway represent a fateful movement from the human to the posthuman precisely because what is at stake in the culture of body drift is a more enduring struggle between the triumphant return of hauntologies of the abject—the religious abject, the technological abject, the political abject—and the quintessentially posthuman determination to make of the contingent, the complex, the hybrid, an insurgency of bodies that do not matter? Of the future of the posthuman body, we can know with certainty only that it is deeply entangled with the different axes of the human condition: sexuality, gender, race, ideology, class, and religion. There are no bodies that have not been stamped with the imprint of class, no subjectivities that do not contain risible traces of ideology, no desires not implicated by the fixed signifiers of gender, no passion that is not circuited through epistemologies of sexuality, no belief that does not bear the visible or, at the minimum, phantom traces of enduring religious controversies and secular rebellions. While the future of the posthuman body can no more be predicted with any certainty than the posthuman future itself, one thing remains definite. Our multiple bodies, our breached genders, our indeterminate sexualities, our nameless pleasures, our proliferating identities will always follow pathways into the future figured by the contingent, the complex, and the hybrid. Consequently, in a future of body drift, Butler, Hayles, and Haraway rise beyond their customary places as exemplary theoreticians to represent something else entirely, namely, creators of a brilliant form of thought that in its formal structure and manifest content constitutes the once and future arc of body drift itself.

NOTES

1. Body Drift

1 Wendy Brown, *States of Injury: Power and Freedom in Late Modernity* (Princeton, N.J.: Princeton University Press, 1995).

2 Throughout the manuscript, I refer to N. Katherine Hayles as Katherine Hayles.

3 Donna Haraway, *The Companion Species Manifesto: Dogs, People, and Significant Otherness* (Chicago: Prickly Paradigm Press, 2003).

4 Judith Butler, *Gender Trouble: Feminism and the Subversion of Identity* (New York: Routledge, 1999); Butler, *Bodies That Matter: On the Discursive Limits of "Sex"* (New York: Routledge, 1993).

5 Judith Butler, *Antigone's Claim: Kinship between Life and Death* (New York: Columbia University Press, 2000); Butler, *The Psychic Life of Power: Theories in Subjection* (Palo Alto, Calif.: Stanford University Press, 1997); Butler, *Giving an Account of Oneself* (New York: Fordham University Press, 2005); Butler, *Precarious Life: The Powers of Mourning and Violence* (London: Verso, 2004).

6 N. Katherine Hayles, *Writing Machines* (Cambridge, Mass.: MIT Press, 2002); Hayles, *How We Became Posthuman: Virtual Bodies in Cybernetics, Literature, and Informatics* (Chicago: University of Chicago Press, 1999); Hayles, *My Mother Was a Computer: Digital Subjects and Literary Texts* (Chicago: University of Chicago Press, 2005).

7 "N. Katherine Hayles in Conversation with Arthur Kroker," April 26, 2006, http://pactac.net/pactacweb/web-content/videoscroll4.html#3.

8 Ibid.

9 Ibid.

10 Donna Haraway, *The Haraway Reader* (New York: Routledge, 2004).

11 The entanglement of Heidegger, Marx, and Nietzsche as premonitory theorists of power in posthuman culture has been explored in my earlier book, *The Will to Technology and the Culture of Nihilism: Heidegger, Nietzsche, and Marx* (Toronto, Ont.: University of Toronto Press, 2004).

12 Martin Heidegger, *Basic Writings,* ed. and introduced by David Karrell Krell (San Francisco: Harper, 1993), 243.

2. Contingencies

1 Butler, *Antigone's Claim,* 82.

2 Butler, *Psychic Life of Power,* 50.

3 Ibid., 50–51.

4 Ibid., 67.

5 Ibid., 130.

6 Ibid., 130–31.

7 Ibid., 97.

8 Ibid., 82.

9 Ibid., 104.

10 Ibid., 105.

11 Ibid., 67.

12 Ibid., 68.

13 Ibid.

14 Ibid., 69.

15 Ibid., 66.

16 Butler, *Bodies That Matter,* 228.

17 Luce Irigaray, *To Be Two* (New York: Routledge, 2001), 57.

18 Butler, *Bodies That Matter,* 235–36.

19 Martin Heidegger, *The Question Concerning Technology and Other Essays,* trans. and with an introduction by William Lovitt (New York: Harper and Row, 1977), 48; emphasis added.

20 Butler, *Precarious Life,* 143.

21 Ibid., 151.

3. Complexities

1   Susan Mapstone, "Non-linear Dynamics: The Swerve of the Atom in Lucretius' *De Rerum Natura*," *London Consortium: Humanities and Cultural Studies Programme* (2004–5): 1–13, http://www.londonconsortium.com/wp-content/uploads/2007/02/mapstonestoicsessay.pdf.

2   Ibid., 2.

3   N. Katherine Hayles, *Chaos and Order: Complex Dynamics in Literature and Science* (Chicago: University of Chicago Press, 1991), 3.

4   Ibid., 1.

5   Ibid.

6   Ibid., 4.

7   Ibid., 1–2.

8   Ibid.

9   Ibid., 9.

10   Ibid., 10.

11   Ibid., 8.

12   Ibid.

13   Hayles, *How We Became Posthuman,* 104.

14   Hayles, *My Mother Was a Computer,* 243.

15   Ibid., 244.

16   Ibid., 242.

17   Ibid., 243.

18   Ibid., 242.

19   Martin Heidegger, *Identity and Difference,* trans. and with an introduction by Joan Stambaugh (Chicago: University of Chicago Press, 2002), 69.

20   Ibid., 34.

21   Ibid., 41.

22   Hayles, *My Mother Was a Computer,* 19.

23   Heidegger, *Identity and Difference,* 41.

24   Ibid., 39.

25   Hayles, *My Mother Was a Computer,* 103.

26   Hayles, *Writing Machines,* 10.

27 Ibid., 15.
28 Hayles, *How We Became Posthuman*, 244.
29 Ibid., 153.
30 Ibid., 156.
31 Ibid., 286.
32 Ibid., 286–87.
33 Ibid., 288.

4. Hybridities

1 Sylvia Hui, "Hawking: Space Exploration a Necessity," Associated Press, June 13, 2006, http://www.usatoday.com/tech/science/space/2006-06-13-hawking-humans-space_x.htm.
2 Donna Haraway, *Primate Visions: Gender, Race, and Nature in the World of Modern Science* (New York: Routledge, 1989), 153.
3 Ibid., 153–54.
4 Franz Fanon, *The Wretched of the Earth* (New York: Grove Press, 1977), 236.
5 Haraway, *Primate Visions*, 185.
6 Ibid., 233.
7 Ibid.
8 Ibid., 234.
9 Ibid.
10 Ibid., 153–54.
11 Ibid.
12 Ibid.
13 Ibid., 233.
14 Ibid.
15 Ibid.
16 Ibid., 234.
17 For an important discussion of the risks associated with genomics, see Michael Tyshenko and William Leiss, "Life in the Fast Lane: An Introduction to Genomics Risk," http://www.ctheory.net/articles.aspx?id=443; and William Leiss, "Biotechnology, Religion and the Body," a seminar presentation at the Pacific Centre for Technology and Culture, University of Victoria, February 8, 2005, http://www.pactac.net/pactacweb/web-content/videoscroll1.html#11.

18 http://www.cbsnews.com/stories/2003/10/13/tech/main576405. shtml.

19 Donna Haraway, *Simians, Cyborgs, and Women: The Reinvention of Nature* (New York: Routledge, 1991), 224.

20 Ibid., 201.

21 Ibid., 196.

22 Ibid., 204.

23 Ibid., 204.

24 Ibid., 188.

25 Ibid., 189.

26 Ibid.

27 Ibid., 252n6.

28 Ibid., 211.

29 Ibid., 213–14. Here Haraway follows closely the visionary perspectives of Terry Winograd and Fernando Flores, *Understanding Computers and Cognition: A New Foundation for Design* (Norwood, N.J.: Ablex, 1986).

30 Ibid., 214.

31 Ibid.

32 Ibid., 225.

33 Ibid.

34 Haraway, *Companion Species Manifesto,* 6.

35 Ibid.

36 Ibid.

37 Ibid., 15–16.

38 Ibid., 11.

Epilogue

1 Breaking with the primordial relationship of power and death, Foucault explored the alignment of power and life: "The mechanisms of power are addressed to the body, to life, to what causes it to proliferate, to what reinforces the species, its stamina, its ability to dominate." Michel Foucault, *The History of Sexuality*, vol. 1, *An Introduction* (New York: Pantheon, 1978), 147.

2 George Grant, *Technology and Empire: Perspectives on North America* (Toronto, Ont.: House of Anansi, 1969), 142.

INDEX

(continued from page ii)

Arthur Kroker is Canada Research Chair in Technology, Culture, and Theory; professor of political science; and director of the Pacific Centre for Technology and Culture at the University of Victoria in British Columbia, Canada. He is the author of several books, including, most recently, *Born Again Ideology: Religion, Technology, and Terrorism* and *The Will to Technology and the Culture of Nihilism: Heidegger, Nietzsche, and Marx.*